HAUNTED LIFE ...

UNABLE TO HIDE
KELLY RENEE SCHUTZ

Book 11

What "Am" I Experiencing?

Illustration by Halida Dwi Edyati

Paranormal Encounters
Haunted Life: Unable to Hide

FIRST EDITION
"Book 11"

Dr. Kelly Renee Schutz
Author

Book Series -- Cover Designers and Illustrators

Cover/Illustra:	Brandy Woods .	Canada
Cover/Illustra:	Magdalena Adic	Croatia
Illustrations:	Halida Dwi Edyati	Indonesia
Illustration:	George Patsouras	New York
Illustration:	Katie Wheeler	Minnesota
Illustrations:	Creative Commons	Unknown
Artwork/Photos:	Kelly Schutz	Minnesota

Published by: Paranormal Universal Press, LLC
www.paranormaluniversalpress.com
Email = krschutz1@yahoo.com

Printed by: Kindle Direct Publishing,
Amazon.com

Paranormal Encounters
Haunted Life: Unable to Hide

Correspondence and Book Orders
Paranormal Universal Press, LLC
krschutz1@yahoo.com

ISBN: 9798417967702
Kindle Direct Publishing and Amazon.com

Printed in the United States of America

Disclaimer

This is the eleventh book written in the Paranormal Encounters series. Book 11 continues sharing the author's first-hand accounts of perceived spiritual, paranormal, extraterrestrial, and/or ultra-terrestrial encounters. This edition includes some of the most popular chapters from previous books, few contributor stories, fiction stories as written by the author, and topics of interest. Chapters are illustrated, educational, and include thought-provoking questions.

If you like to read personal accounts involving premonitions, apparitions, awakenings, communicating with unexplained, extraterrestrial visitations, deceased person shape shifting into living human body, neurodivergent disorder association to ESP and to paranormal, sentient anomalies (light beings), energies, hauntings, and moon phases, this book will not disappoint. To entice the reader further, a short introduction about 4-1-1 disappearances will keep your interest.

The exploration of paranormal and extraterrestrial phenomena brings varying reactions - excitement, speculation, and ridicule. Those who have not had an experience with various types of dimensional phenomena are often quick to judge others about their certainties and exploration of it.

To date, the author continues to experience unexplained paranormal-extraterrestrial, and with question, ultra-terrestrial phenomena. *Haunted Life: Unable to Hide* continues where the other books have left off ... a lifetime of unanswered questions.

Stories in this book are illustrated to help the reader visually experience situations from the author's perspective. Some sketches are modified to protect the anonymity of physical locations, situations, and people. Images or stories resembling your own encounters, situations, or actual persons - known, living, or dead - are coincidental. This book, as all the others, showcase author and few contributor experiences.

This book is intended as a form of entertainment. The stories shared in this book are not exaggerations or fake accounts of encounters experienced in unexplained situations. Most stories do not involve (to be best of my intuition) a demonic encounter. Negative or perceived to be demonic encounters illustrate various forms of paranormal or unexplained energy.

Properties mentioned in this book are either private or are advertised to the public as being haunted. The author makes no representations or claims as to the accuracy of these properties "being haunted." Can a person unknowingly haunt a property? Yes. Will the haunting remain once departed? Not necessarily.

The author does believe each of her personal encounters involved unexplained paranormal or extraterrestrial activity. While it is exciting to explore and capture such activities, a beginning ghost seeker should always take proper steps to respect private property while adhering to trespassing laws.

Always seek permission when exploring a private property. Do not trespass as it is against the law and can be dangerous to you, your friends, or your family [physically and emotionally].

Dedications

I would like to dedicate this book to my husband, family, friends, and those who share my passion in exploring the paranormal and ufology fields. My motivation in trying to find answers to my unexplained encounters is often put to task by skeptics.

I would also like to thank my husband for his tolerance in my enthusiasm in chasing unknown phenomena by spending most of our vacations at haunted locations to help me determine whether paranormal and extraterrestrial situations do exist.

Finally, thank you to the little girl and older man, who I photographed in an upper screened window at what was once my father's – grandfather's – and built by my great grandfather's home on May 6, 2007. The clarity of their features along with their expressions of puzzlement in looking directly at me sparked a question in my mind to revisit the property to which I telepathically heard, "check the genealogy" section in my family history identifying the young gal. Her name was incorrect.

Capturing their images not only turned my disbelief about ghosts into the realization that some not only existed but visit their former homes. However, were these apparitions who I thought they were? Or "demonic" tricksters lowering my guard?

Thank you to my book series illustrative team - Brandy Woods (cover designer-illustrator, Canada), Magdalena Adic (cover designer-illustrator, Croatia), Halida Dwi Edyati (Illustrator, Indonesia), George Patsouras (illustrator, New York), Katie Wheeler (illustrator, Minnesota), Unknown (Creative Commons), and others as hired for helping me to visually tell my stories.

Table of Contents
Haunted Life: Unable to Hide

Illustration by Kelly Renee Schutz

Table of Contents

Disclaimer iii

Dedications v

Author, Cover Designer, Illustrators ix

Author Experienced Phenomena and Psi xvii

Introduction 1

Books Written 7

Investigation Preparation Log 9

Protection Prayers 10

Chapter 1: Early Years: Premonitions 11

Chapter 2: Behind the Curtain 19

Chapter 3: Psychic Warns of Powerful Mind 40

Chapter 4: Faces in the Window Screen 46

Chapter 5: Tales of Apparitions #1: The Tree Swing 58

Chapter 6: Poltergeist 64

Chapter 7: Prince Rupert Hotel – Cycling Mirror 85

Chapter 8: Spiritual, Para-, Extra- or Ultra-terrestrial 120

Chapter 9: Waking Up Clothes Backwards 127

Chapter 10: Tales of Apparitions #2: Twinberry Lane 133

Chapter 11: Blood Red Handprint 137

Chapter 12: Fisherman Manifests on Boat 149

Chapter 13: Nanteos Mansion Country House 154

Chapter 14: Tales of Apparitions #3: Deadwillow M 180

Chapter 15: Deceased Shape-Shifts into Living Body 188

Chapter 16: Neurodivergent Beacon 196

Table of Contents
(continued)

Chapter 17: Tales of Apparitions #4: Bezzle Lake   207

Chapter 18: Energies That Attract Ghosts   214

Chapter 19: Hauntings and Types of Ghosts   234

Chapter 20: Moon Phases and Energy Fields   246

Chapter 21: One Thump or Two   249

Chapter 22: Tales of Apparitions #5: Old Firebug   255

Chapter 23: Attacked in Haunted Museum   260

Chapter 24: Lady Catherine   288

Chapter 25: Haunted Jerome Grand Hotel   293

Chapter 26: UFOs and Abduction Theory   320

Chapter 27: 4-1-1 Disappearances   324

Guest Appearances, Interviews, and Features   327

Book Covers (1-11)   329

Radio Shows   340

Paranormal Phenomena Snips (Books 1-9)   341

Music Composers   346

IF PURCHASING AS A COMBO
PURCHASE TOGETHER WITH THIS INFORMATION

BOOK 9 and 10   [12 chapters are repetitive]

BOOK 9 and 11   [3 chapters are repetitive]

BOOK 10 and 11   [5 chapters are repetitive]

Author
and
Designing Team

AUTHOR/COVER   COVER/SKETCHES

ILLUSTRATORS and FORMER COVER ARTIST

Author
Dr. Kelly Renee Schutz

Dr. Kelly Renee Schutz is a retired college professor who once specialized in applied communications, human relationships, and management. Her lifelong interests have included the understanding of differences among people with a secondary interest in exploring paranormal and ufology phenomena. A paranormal enthusiast, she uses her intuition and extra sensory perception skills to guide her in understanding unexplained situations. She is currently the host-producer of two highly ranked paranormal podcast shows heard worldwide, author-publisher, speaker, photographer, crafter-artist, voice actor, registered cottage baker, cookbook creator, genealogist, and world traveler. Academically, she earned five advanced degrees including paralegal litigation (investigative). She currently has six freelance businesses (artist-crafter, voice actor, cottage baker, paranormal book writer, podcaster, and cookbook creator) and is a leader of five art groups with Fine Art America. In 2021, she was interviewed by ABC Network television producers to be a contestant on a new game show.

Artist and Illustrator
Brandy Woods, Canada

Brandy Woods is an award-winning visual illustrator who specializes in Native American-inspired and fantasy themes. She enjoys painting and sculpture. While she doesn't personally have status, a distant grandmother was full-blooded Choctaw and she was raised with a deep love and respect for the First Nations. She graduated with honors from Dawson College's prestigious Illustration and Design program. She grew up in Louisiana and spent much of her childhood reading Wendy Pini's 'ElfQuest', as well as numerous books on mythology, shamanism, fantasy, and other cultures. She has long dreamed of illustrating books, to inspire a new generation of dreamers. Brandy was contracted for this multi-book project to showcase her life-sketching talents. Recommended artist of **upwork.com**. Here work can be seen at **www.brandywoods.com**.

Illustrator (Sketches)
Halida Dwi Edyati, Surabaya, Indonesia

Halida Dwi Edyati is a professional digital sketch illustrator. I selected her from "Fiverr.com" to create sketches for this book. She is a passionate, skilled, and detail-concerned artist who demonstrates dedication to her projects.

Her career in art design and illustration began in 2015. She studied at the Institut Teknologi Sepuluh Nopember, a school located in Indonesia.

In 2020, she launched her talent to the world by showcasing her remarkable skills in digital painting, illustrating, and pencil sketching.

A recommended artist of **Fiverr.com.**

Former Cover Artist-Illustrator
Magdalena Adic, Zagreb, Croatia

Magdalena Adic was born in Croatia, a country in southeastern Europe. She studied wood technology processing at the University of Zagreb, Faculty of Forestry and graduated with all prescribed rights in 2012. As a graphic designer, she started working in 2015, out of love for aided design and art. Magdalena custom designs print and eBook covers, using photo manipulation, digital art, and illustration. She is also an expert in package design. Other areas of expertise include logo design, branding, website design, and conceptual art. To date, she has worked on more than 156 projects in the field of graphic design, published a book under the pseudonym "The Author" and published a collection of contemporary art works through Fine Art America. Recommended artist of **upwork.com**. Also view work: **http://www.coroflot.com/magdalena_adic**.

Illustrator (Sketch)
George Patsouras, New York

George Patsouras currently lives in Long Island City, New York. He began developing his artistic skills at a young age. As a child, he was inspired to draw everything from comics to Greek Mythology. Then, his favorite medium was using pencils. Now, an established artist, he combines a variety of media techniques using pencils and digital painting. A freelance artist (with much success), he has risen to becoming established in illustration arts. Many of his works can be seen on numerous publications – ranging from board games to card games. His work can also be seen on various book covers. George loves creating artwork and it shows in personal artistic style/expression. George was contracted to prepare an illustrative sketch for this book. He is a recommended artist of **upwork.com.**

Illustrator (Sketch)
Katie Wheeler, Minneapolis, Minnesota

Katie Wheeler was born in southern Minnesota. She currently works as a design engineer. She graduated from the College of Design at the University of Minnesota, Minneapolis. She would consider herself to be a visual artist who likes to illustrate using oils, paints, acrylics, and pencils. At the age of five years old, she began working with paints and pencils discovering her love for art. Bringing her images to life, she has provided sketches for two books, one that is a personal biography and the other, a published book made into a series. Her artwork has been sold as greeting and notecards in hobby stores as well as a contribution to raise money to help kids afford art supplies at a premier art gallery near Chicago, Illinois. Katie likes to listen to music, travel, and go to art museums.

What Not To Say To A Ghost
"Bring It On"

Illustration by George Patsouras

Phenomena and Psi

The author has experienced MOST of these phenomena and unexplained situations for over 50+ years. ** = Not yet. Spontaneous human combustion (rare, real phenomena).

Afterlife Communication

Alien Abduction-Visitation

Angels

Animal Apparitions-Connection

Anomalies

Apport [Objects]

Attachments

Bigfoot**

Black-Eyed Children/Teens

Brain Frequency Changes

Cemeteries [Chatter]

Channeling**

Clairaudient

Clairsentient

Clairvoyant

Communication with Apparitions

Consciousness

Cryptids**

Curses

Demons

Déjà vu

Deport [Objects]

Disturbed Ground

Dreams

Dying

Ectoplasmic Orbs/Mists

Electromagnetic Effects

Elementals**

Energy Forms

Energetic Signature

ESP

Hag Syndrome

Handprints [Body and Objects]

Haunted Cemeteries

Haunted Objects

Human Hybridization**

Imprints

Intelligent Haunting

Intention

Interdimensional-Multi-Dimensional**

Intuition

Ley Lines

Mandela Effect

Manifestation

Memory-Time Loss

Mothman

Near Death

Negative Attraction

Night Terrors

Out of Body**

Orbs

Past Life Regression

Phasmophobia

Poltergeist

Portals

Possession

Psychic Ability

Psychokinesis

Reincarnation

Remote Viewing

Residual Haunting

Scratched

Shadow People [white and black]

Séance

Sentient Beings

Skinwalker**

Slender Man**

Spells-Wishes

Starseed People

Synchronicity

Tarot and Smoke Readings

Telekinesis

Teleportation**

Thanatophobia

Time Slips**

Touched by Unseen Entities

Trance

Trauma

Trigger Object

UFO [metal vessel and light orb anomalies]**

Visions-Visual Flashes

Introduction

This is Book 11 in the Paranormal Encounters book series. This book continues sharing author encounters, few contributor stories, popular chapters from previous books, fiction stories as written by the author, topics-of-interest, and discussion.

My having a discussion with people about ghosts brings many types of responses. Reactions have varied from fear to disbelief regarding their existence and is often followed by one of these comments, "if ghosts exist, then, why haven't I seen or encountered one?" "Where is this ghost in which you speak of?" "Here, ghostie, ghostie, ha-ha." Or "I think you need to see a shrink because your brain cells are malfunctioning – he-he." I learned a long time ago that it is pointless to try to convince someone who has never had a paranormal encounter that ghosts do exist. Some people have experiences, and some do not. If you have not, when the time comes ... you will know it.

The subject of ghosts is not a "top five" water cooler topic either. Have you ever heard someone say during a lunch break, "so, was your pesky ghost behaving itself last night?" or "full moon tonight – BOO." Most people are uncomfortable discussing this topic and have tendencies to change the subject quickly by ignoring it, expressing a reaction, or remaining silent. In a verbal poll I conducted a few years ago amongst a diverse group of people, it was found that about 84% not only believed in ghosts but felt they had a personal encounter with one. About 11% were skeptical about them but expressed their being afraid to experience an event for fear of encountering something demonic. And, about 5% felt ghosts did not exist concluding in their minds that the stories people shared were either made up in their heads, imagined, or contrived.

Why do some people have experiences and others do not? This is not an easy question to answer. My responses generally lean in the direction of sensitivity, timing [chance], ignoring cues, attitude, brain frequency, mental disorders, ground disturbance, environmental and weather conditions, moon phases, or personal beliefs [religious] about the afterlife.

It is RARE that one can easily "call out" or "see" a ghost on verbal request. On occasion, I have had this ability to do so given the right conditions. However, many people are not so fortunate to experience a ghost, leading to disappointment or the questioning of their existence. If a floor squeaks, does this mean a ghost is present? Maybe this sound is an imprint or is due to a temperature change in the environment. A wall bangs or knocks ... does this mean a ghost is trying to gain your attention? Or maybe the pipes are expanding and clanking. A dead clock hands move to different times of the day during new and full moon phases. Is this a battery malfunction, weather change, or home electrical issue? Could any of these situations mean a ghost is present? Possibly. EMF levels out of whack?

Those who are overly sensitive have what is called a *third eye* or **sixth sensory sense.** A **sixth sensory sense** is best described as a psychic radar (sensitive to the observation of cues) that most people do not readily see or just ignore. Some have a higher frequency or radiate as a beacon of light. Most would agree that watching for or paying too much attention to unusual cues in their surroundings is not only exhausting but a waste of time and energy often leading to a form of paranoia. Trying to summon a ghost can lead to energy drain and false hallucinations.   2

Since the age of nine, I became aware I had a *sixth sensory sense*. Today, I would just tell you that my frequency is higher than most. You may have heard about situations of children playing with an imaginary friend. I never had such a playmate, but my husband did at the age of 3. Children are "highly sensitive" and intuitive before age of 6. Although their abilities are more sensitive around this age, it is not uncommon to hear experiences occurring between the ages of 6-14.

At age 3, my husband played alone most of the time. One day, his mother asked him who he was playing with, to which he responded, "Bob." It just so happens he had a deceased brother by the name of "Robert" [passed away before he was born] however, the name of this child was never revealed to him until age 50. It was by accident he found out his brother's name when he overheard a conversation between his mother and me (mumbling in the kitchen). Coincidence? Perhaps. In this situation, it was more likely he was playing with his deceased uncle, named Robert, who was his mother's brother.

Nevertheless, not all imaginary play friends are "ghost" encounters. Not all children see or have ghost playmates. In most cases, parents believe their child will grow out of their imaginary play friend stage as they get older because a child's sensitivity to cues in their surroundings desensitize over time.

My fascination with the afterlife grew to a heightened level after the discovery of my photographing two ghost faces in the upper window screen of my paternal grandparents' farmhouse on May 6, 2007. This image appears in this book [Faces in the Window Screen]. Since that day, my attitude about this image continues to wonder ... were these apparitions of my relatives or something more devious? 3

Before May 2007, I would have unexplained moments of anxiousness in situations causing me distress or stomach aches (often passed off as hormonal changes or depression).

Many of you might be able to relate ... at an early age, I was never a fan of going upstairs alone, opening closed doors, walking down into dark basements, etc. I have no idea why. Not alone in feeling this way, my three-year old nephew refused to go into his home basement by himself or into my paternal grandparents' barn (haunted) that was 150 feet away from the farmhouse (very haunted). When asked why not, he had a hard time explaining his resistance. Was he experiencing a "sixth sensory sense" or are these situations just "unfamiliar"?

In my teens, I continually wished I could see a ghost. People always talked about them, but I felt I wasn't fortunate enough to have an experience. My wish to see a ghost (relayed out loud while walking alone on my paternal grandparent's farm property in my teens) came without warning on May 6, 2007.

The home, built by my paternal great grandfather and passed down to my grandfather and father, survived a straight-line tornado force wind that ripped through the property knocking over a 150-year old tree onto a live powerline. On May 5, 2007, this weather event not only shook the house but caused a manifestation of who I believe are the images of two of my deceased family members (showed in a screened window). In doing research, the young gal, believed to be my great aunt (father's side), died in my great grandfather's first of four homes (rental) two miles away. The older man, believed to be my paternal great grandfather, passed away in a hospital but had a strong attachment to his home and property.

My great grandparents had lived in three homes in the same area before building their fourth home, a very grand home, with his own hands and relatives around years 1901-1904. The day I visited the farm property (post-tornado), it had not occurred to me that I was being watched by someone[s] in an upper screened window. On this day, the weather conditions were overcast, a bitterly cold feeling resonating throughout the air, still breeze, birds chirping, and the sound of an electrical charge radiating from the downed tree onto a powerline and into the air. A limestone foundation under the home acted as a conductor for creating energy, possibly charged from the storm's lightning strikes. What I did not realize then was these conditions became the perfect recipe for manifestation of visible apparitions. Electricity is energy for manifestations.

Most ghost hunting enthusiasts know the five basic rules: (1) protect yourself (wear or hold a cross and say a protection prayer), (2) show respect to the deceased, (3) understand your reasons for seeking ghosts, (4) know when to leave them alone, and (5) respect private property. It is best to ask for permission before entering a premise. It can be quite exciting to capture a paranormal anomaly; but do so with good practice, not wrong practice. Wearing a cross will not always protect you.

From personal experience, ghosts come and leave quickly, often working on their own schedules. Most visual manifestations (orb, mist, appearance) last 3-5 seconds. Ghosts generally reveal themselves to one person, not to pairs or groups. A ghost's cooperation with you will depend on a variety of circumstances as well as their comfort in being around you. Warning to the curious ... you may bring home an attachment.

I do not consider myself to be psychic. I would call myself a sensitive intuitive empath with a high frequency (beacon of light) who is able to sequence together unexplained coincidences or cues when in haunted situations (some) or in places where someone has passed wanting to share a message.

I believe, my being open about their existence is what attracts them to me with 99.5% of my experiences being non-threatening. Not all situations provide "a message."

Although the goal of this book is to entertain and share with you my personal real-life stories, it is also designed to give further insight into paranormal topics-perceived encounters. It is my hope to help you become a better observer when investigating unexplained situations that typically defy the laws naturalism.

Experiencing a paranormal event can happen at any age and can be life changing. For some, the thrill of discovering a "ghost" can be elating – for others, it is plain and simple ... terrifying.

Whether you are a believer or not ... here is where your journey about this phenomenon evolves or ends.

Dr. Kelly Renee Schutz

Books Written

BOOK 1

Paranormal Encounters: Attacks, Manifestations, Attachments, Poltergeists [4 Topics, 12 Non-Fiction Stories]
235 Pages (Illustrated)

BOOK 2

Paranormal Encounters: Be Careful What You Wish For
[4 Topics, 12 Non-Fiction Stories]
254 Pages (Illustrated)

BOOK 3

Paranormal Encounters: Beyond the Grave
[24 Non-Fiction, Stories Combined from Books 1 and 2]
306 Pages (Illustrated)

BOOK 4

Paranormal Encounters: Defying Naturalism
[14 Theory Topics and 2 Non-Fiction Bonus Chapters]
202 Pages (Illustrated)

BOOK 5

Paranormal Encounters: Hanging Around
[20 Non-Fiction, 5 Fiction, Haunted Locations/B&B]
318 Pages (Illustrated)

BOOK 6

Paranormal Encounters: Through A Child's Eyes
[16 Non-Fiction, 2 Fiction, 6 Adult Stories Bonus Chapters]
160 Pages (Shortened Perspectives of Children and Adult)

BOOK 7
Paranormal Encounters: Haunted Phenomena
[70+ Non-Fiction (Shortened Stories); Compiled from Books 1-6]
200 Pages (Illustrated)

BOOK 8
Paranormal Encounters: Investigative Journal (Notebook)

BOOK 9
Paranormal Encounters: Manifestations
[30 Non-Fiction, 1 Fiction; Compiled from Books 1-3 and 5]
381 Pages (Illustrated)

BOOK 10
Paranormal Encounters: Message Received
[20 Non-Fiction, Few Contributor and Some Previous Books]
363 Pages (Illustrated)

BOOK 11
Haunted Life: Unable to Hide
[18 Non-Fiction (Some Previous), 5 Fiction Stories, 4 Topics of Interest]
383 Pages (Illustrated)

Life Moves Along
The Journey Continues

Investigation Preparation Log

☐ Research of the location completed. Interviews of the subjects completed.

☐ Received permissions to go onto the location or site.

☐ Assembled a small investigation team.

☐ All equipment fully charged with back-up accessories.

☐ Understands hazards involved. Bring face masks for poor air quality or molds; wear proper footwear and jacket. Etc.

☐ All to be wearing a holy cross. Say protection prayer. Be conscious of unusual physical reactions. Sage stick.

☐ Bring notebook or audio recorder to take notes to debunk situations and record unusual events.

☐ Bring trigger objects if you intend to use them.

☐ Your software is advanced enough to review EVPs or watch video tapings for analysis.

☐ Follow-up with client to review findings or set up another time for a 2nd or 3rd investigation of location.

☐ Sage yourself and team members to remove unwanted attachments.

Protection Prayers

ALWAYS PROTECT YOURSELF

When spirit adventuring, it is important you wear or carry a cross or religious/spiritual object, say a protection prayer, and surround yourself with white light to create a safety shield from harmful entities. Say prayer before bedtime in haunted location.

SIGN OF THE CROSS with or without HOLY WATER

"In the name of the Father and of the Son and of the Holy Spirit. Amen." [Dabble water on forehead, dabble down to the middle of your chest, dabble across to the front of the left shoulder, and dabble across to the front of the right shoulder]. Forms the sign of a cross over body. "Peace to this house and all who dwell within it." [Sprinkle water in room; show no fear; feel the words you say].

WHITE LIGHT PROTECTION PRAYER

I call upon the white light of protection to come forth from the golden orb above my head, covering my entire body from the top of my head to the bottom of my feet, through each chakra extending through my entire aura. This white light surrounds, protects, heals, and guides me, going within to further protect, cleanse, purify and heal, totally permeating my entire being. I ask any and all negative, sickly, jealous, evil, or mean energies, entities, spirits, guides, or vibrations that have attached themselves to me or are within my presence be sent back to their source, never to return to seek me out. I ask this blessing with neither love nor hate, but for sake of the greatest good. In the name of the almighty, I thank you.

Messages

I may appear alone but I am in a place that gives me comfort.

Illustration by Magdalena Adic

All I did was show I could cycle my mirror around.

Illustration by Brandy Woods

It didn't' take much for us to expand into a mist and fly through a solid wooden door.

Illustration by Brandy Woods

I was just looking out for your best interest (missed by an inch).

Illustration by Brandy Woods

Chapter 1
Early Years: Premonitions

Airplane Crash
Weather Events
Civil Unrest Situations

Illustration by Halida Dwi Edyati

Chapter 1
Early Years: Premonitions

ABILITIES AWAKENING

From the beginning. I believe my extra sensory perception abilities (ESP) were sparked within me around age 3 but awakened by age 4. When you are a child, unusual coincidences are just that ... coincidences.

THE EARLY YEARS

I don't recall much growing up before age 4. My upbringing began in Minnesota and Louisiana. Around age 3, startling situations began etching into my memory.

LOUISIANA

A few months before I turned ONE years old, my father uprooted our family leaving Minnesota and moving to Rosepine, Louisiana. He was to be stationed at an Army boot camp just outside of Rosepine, a small town mixed with culture. Being months old, I recall nothing.

My mother, brother (one year older), and I joined him after he settled into boot camp. We traveled there from Minnesota in a car that was in need of constant attention every 100 miles (for 1600 miles). After numerous stops to keep the car in motion, we eventually arrived in Rosepine settling into a small rental house occupied by a Hispanic couple.

Louisiana

According to the U.S. Census, between 1950 and 1969, the population of Rosepine was approximately 350-414 people. Poor community.

Our family of four shared a one-level rambler home with a Hispanic couple who loved making Mexican food (daily) (strong smelling). The couple lived on one side of the house, and we lived on the other side. We shared a common kitchen. I do not believe there was much conversation as my parents knew no Spanish nor they English. Sign language served its purposes. While in Rosepine, I was too young to recall any memory there.

MOVING BACK TO MINNESOTA

After my father completed training, we moved back to Minnesota. We moved into an older two-story home situated on a piece of land just outside of a small town. My grandparents (maternal) lived in town (convenient, two miles away).

LITTLE WHITE HOUSE

Our property, as I recall, had a large grassy yard, trees, clothesline, garden, dog, farm animals, and an open-door barn-shed (dark, empty). I always ran through the barn-shed because its darkness within gave me the creeps. The barn-shed was a short distance from the house. An active railroad train track resided behind it. Several feet down our driveway to the right was a busy grain elevator with trucks coming and going. And, within a half mile on the other side of our house was a lake-swamp. This lake-swamp posed a flooding threat to our house every Spring. To this day, we refer to that home as, "the Pewee house."

RAILROAD HITCH HIKERS

The dangers of living on this property were everywhere. The train track brought with it bums (train car hitch hikers or walkers) daily. These bums would stop, knock on our door, and beg for something to eat. My mother, out of fear, would make them a sandwich to avoid questionable confrontations. adverse behaviors, or kid abductions.

As a side note: I cannot recall this story exactly but during a trip to the Amana Colonies, Iowa, my husband and I stayed at Huber's Bed and Breakfast. We were told back in the day, their property was near or part of an active train terminal that transported thousands of people to their destinations. This property had an active hotel.

The owners stated railroad train hitch hikers would "mark" houses and posts in route indicating which were "food friendly" in providing a meal or food. A form of indirect communication.

Although I am not sure if a "mark" was etched onto the "pewee house" (not by us) or post enroute, one thing became apparent ... my mother didn't want confrontation with the hitch hikers and walkers. She simply awaited the predictable knock on the door and provided a sandwich.

DEATH SPARKS SENSORY

I was 3 years old when my baby brother passed away suddenly from SIDS. As a young child, his unusual and untimely death left me confused.   My parents, however, were traumatized.

What traumatized me in this situation wasn't sadness from the learning of his death. My trauma resulted from visually "seeing" and "feeling" the acts of my parent's pain.

My parents didn't want my older brother or I to attend my brother's funeral. They felt we would be in the way. We were brought to my grandparent's house for care. I never received closure from his death. Or would I at age 3?

FLOOD FORCES EVACUATION

As if railroad hitch hikers, an active grain elevator, and a death in the family wasn't hard enough to deal with, now comes Spring when our home is threatened by dangerous flooding.

I remember "fleeing day" as if it were yesterday. Flood waters were rising steadily covering all four corners of our yard. My mother knew we were in trouble when she opened the trap door to the basement and discovered a cat-sized rat at the top of the stairs with nothing but water underneath it. The sheriff stopped by to tell us we needed to evacuate. We grabbed our stuff and rushed to the car. I was sitting in the back seat awaiting my father to return from the house to drive us off the property. He seemed to be taking a long time. As a three-year old, all you think about is your dying from situations like these. Trauma.

At the point my father returned, once the car door opened, water gushed inside hitting my feet. I screamed inside my head, "let's get out of here!" Or were these words spoken outside my head. Of course, my father was having a difficult time starting the car (never ran properly). It simply would not turn over. The longest ten minutes of fright one could ever endure. Trauma.

As a side note: Flooding caused a horrid, lake-swamp smell on this property. This horrid smell is why we referred to that little white house as "the pewee house."

NEW OWNER

The "pewee house" should have been torn down after that flood. It was under so much swamp water the boards swelled and rotted.

The owner of the house decided to clean it up and re-rent it to a physician by the name of Dr. Sexy (yes, real name). Maybe Dr. Sexy was looking for a cheap, temporary place to live while he served his medical residency. He found it.

As an interesting side note, years later, I would be knocking on Dr. Sexy's house door asking him if he were interested in purchasing light bulbs (4-H fundraiser). "No thanks," he said.

I don't know why but the excitement of returning to that home sent shivers up my spine and made my heart race. I wasn't allowed to go inside but he gave me a good look from the door into the kitchen.

As an older adult, I would like to have gone back to that house to revisit its internal design and go back upstairs to the bedroom where I slept. They say, you leave a piece of your energy in every place you reside. I wonder if Dr. Sexy ever felt ours.

The house has since been torn down and the property continues to flood every year. When I drive by that property (occasionally), I only see my past there.

DEFINITIONS

Coincidence – concurrence of events or circumstances without apparent causal connection. **Reaction** - an action performed or a feeling experienced in response to a situation or event. **Sensitive** - the ability to perceive information through extra sensory perception (ESP). **Empath** – a person with the paranormal ability to apprehend the mental or emotional state of another individual. **Trauma** – a deeply distressing or disturbing experience, such as the death of a child. **Trigger** – activating feelings experienced in the past.

QUESTIONS AND THOUGHTS

I have always wanted to ask my mother if she ever noticed me (as a child) being intuitively psychic in my abilities. As of this writing, I am able to look back at my life to recognize portions of it deemed "unexplainable."

In reviewing the words my mother wrote about me in my baby book, she mentioned I was an independent thinker and stubborn. I would say these words hold true to this day. When I put my mind to something – watch out.

Because my mother is religious (raised Catholic, converted to Lutheran at marriage), she is and has always remained skeptical of extra sensory perception abilities (ESP). Per my question above in Paragraph 1, I doubt she would admit to anything about my abilities.

18

Chapter 2
Behind the Curtain

Illustration by Brandy Woods
Updated Story as Published in Previous Books

Chapter 2
Behind the Curtain

THE AWAKENING

I feel my senses began to awaken around age 4 and heightened by age 9. Particularly when staying at my "maternal" grandparent's house alone after school.

PHENOMENA

You feel something is residing behind a closed curtain. You hear sounds of laughter (chatter) coming from the kitchen. You smell something decomposing in a room and become overwhelmed with illness. You are attacked by something in this room you cannot see. A music box starts to play without it being touched. A jar containing baby teeth jumps out in front of you falling over on a table. A curtain located on the second level of the house catches on fire but extinguishes itself. A tornado wind hits the house causing damage but not enough to condemn it.

Do I believe my former grandparent's home was haunted and protected by "something" who did not like house guests? Yes.

BRIEF HISTORY

Prior to my grandparents taking ownership of this home, it was reported that a previous owner, a woman, was burned to death by a fire in a porch adjacent to the kitchen. It is my belief this woman was not ready to leave her home and was angry with anyone who visited there. Theorists would say this entity was territorial. I would say this entity was demonic.

My grandparents were strong Catholic believers whose faith did not engage in ideas about a "paranormal afterlife." In fact, in a few brief discussions with my grandmother, I recall asking her if she ever thought her house was haunted. She just giggled and told me it was not haunted and to get that idea out of my head. After my experiencing unforeseen forces in her home, I respectfully disagree.

TRAGIC INCIDENTS

When "something" appears to hang around a specific location after their death has occurred, it seems as though we want to believe that this "something" is or was a former resident. Theories suggest people who pass away suddenly from tragic incidents such as murder, violent crime, suicide, tragic accident, or unexpected death (overdose, illness) may not know their soul has moved out of their physical body and continue to participate in life as if they never left it.

Others, who have passed on may be: (1) unwilling or unable to crossover to an astral plane, (2) could be watching over their loved ones or property, or in some cases, (3) are lost or stuck on earth not knowing how to depart from it. What about "afterlife" agendas?

DEFINITIONS

Apparition or entity – a spirit that has a soul, consciousness, or mind, surviving the death of its body capable of interacting with the living (may be seen, heard, felt, or smelled). **Astral plane** - a world believed to exist above our physical world. **Attack** – a feeling of weakness, low energy, dizzy, sick stomach, ill, or overcome by strong or rotting smells, such as deceased animals or strong scents.

Clairaudience - an auditory form of ESP paranormal information that is received outside the range of normal perception through hearing voices, whispers, and auditory impressions. **Coincidence** – concurrence of events or circumstances without apparent causal connection.

False awakening - an event where the person thinks they are alert or awake, but they are really dreaming. **Sensitive** - the ability to perceive information through extrasensory perception (ESP). **Subjective apparition** - a hallucination of apparitions or other phenomena created in our minds. **Telekinesis** – ability to control one's physical environment without using physical manipulation or force.

Trigger – activating feelings experienced in the past. **Trigger Object** – a person or object used to cause or elicit reactions from unseen energies [ghosts].

THE ENCOUNTERS

OVERLY SENSITIVE. My former grandparent's home was built around 1898. They took possession of it around 1955-56. This would be their second home in the same town. Between the ages of 9 and 17, I would have days when I would need to stay at their home alone while they were out running errands or on vacation. Their home was known as a safe place to go for my siblings and myself, a place where we stayed when babysat, ill, spent time with them, or waited for our mother to pick us up after school.

During my afternoon stayovers at this home (alone), I would feel anxious or nervous. My excuse in feeling nervous, I believed then, was due to an unfamiliar environment causing me anxiety. Was I experiencing anxiety or "something" else?

To combat my anxiety of being there alone, I would wander the first-floor rooms, watch television, sing, talk out loud, or try to nap to pass the time away. On some occasions, I would sense unexplained moments of feeling anxious often escalating into panic attacks. Panic attacks where I would start to physically perspire. As I aged, I thought my **sensitivities** to being there would lessen. However, my anxiousness would appear to intensify leading to more sweating or stomach aches.

QUESTIONS AND THOUGHTS

Unfamiliar homes, buildings, and spaces, regardless of age, seem to captivate overactive imaginations making most anxious people feel threatened by its environment. Was I experiencing anxiety or a **subjective apparition** in this home? No.

Was I <u>unable</u> to grow out of my feeling nervous being in this house alone even at an older age? Unable? At any age, I was never able to grow out of my feeling uneasy, panicked, anxious, paranoid, watched, and moments filled with uncertainties.

THE KITCHEN LAUGHTER. All houses – old or new – have their noises and construction settling quirks. Built around 1898, few renovations were made to this home with most updates being made to the outside exterior. This home appeared to have no hidden secrets. In the basement lie a dirt floor (unfinished) and would be visited often by my grandfather who cleaned his catch of the day (fish) in a sink down there. A wooden floor (2nd story floor) would squeak when stepped on, typical of old plank floors.

One day, while I was in the house alone, I decided to take a nap to combat my feeling anxious. A few hours into my nap, I would awaken to hear loud noises, mumble, and laughter coming from the kitchen. Thinking I must have been out of it to not hear my grandparents return, in a sleepy daze, I proceeded to wander to the kitchen.

As I approached the doorway leading into the kitchen, the loud talking and laughter would suddenly stop. Looking into an empty kitchen, my eyes would gaze intently at the table ... and then ... look to the door leading down into the basement ... and then ... look out the window. I saw no human existence. Confused and with my heart racing, I wandered with hesitation back to the couch to finish my nap while breaking out in a nervous, unsettling sweat.

What just happened to me? Where did these noises come from? Am I hallucinating?

QUESTIONS AND THOUGHTS

The sounds of laughter and noises awakened me from my nap. Did I just sense a moment being **clairaudient** yet finding no one in the kitchen? Yes. Or did I experience a **false awakening**? No. Those who pass tragically at a location (the kitchen) may return to it as the setting may be of most comfort to them. The mumbling, laughter, and noise created from the kitchen was loud enough to wake me up. Not finding anyone in the kitchen (dead silent) brought about sweating and suspicious reaction from me.

AFTER THE INCIDENT. After the kitchen laughter incident occurred, I would find myself on "alone days" either sitting in their bathroom with the doors closed (they had two doors) or in their sun porch (cold or hot weather), with the door leading inside to the house locked (by me) (see images, page 39).

In absolute emergencies, I would go inside to use the bathroom or telephone. When asked why I would sit in the sun porch and not go inside, I would make excuses by saying something to effect that it was unnerving being inside the house.

Of course, the reaction back to me was, "that's crazy, what's wrong with you" ... "there's nothing in the house to be afraid of." In my mind though, "yes, there was." Years later ... "YES" ... there was.

My feelings of uneasiness continued to escalate every time I stayed there alone. I thought I could overcome these feelings as I grew older. No. As I briefly did before, I would ask my grandmother if she thought her house was haunted. To which I would get another stunned reaction, "that's nonsense."

I was now convinced that my fear being in that house alone was nothing more than my imagination getting the best of me. When I found myself having moments of anxiety, I would go right back to what I did before -- turn the volume up on the television, turn all the lights on, sing loudly, talk non-stop, keep the inside door from the house to the sun porch open, sit alone in the bathroom with both doors closed, and sometimes, would leave the house and sit outside on the steps. Paranoid? I could never overcome this feeling.

CLOSED CURTAIN. Perhaps what frightened me the most was the closed curtain at the top of the stairs that led up to the second floor. With its heavy, dark material used to keep the cold and heat air drafts behind it, I would suffer from anxiety with every step I took until I reached the top before grabbing it and pulling it open. Add to this heart stopping moment, the musky scent the curtain gave off because it hung so long without being washed. Do we now have a smell sensation engaging my fear?

GRANDMOTHER PASSES. Years began to pass and my visits to my grandparent's home lessened. Eventually, I would grieve the loss of my grandmother (nearly 90 years old), who suffered from a deadly stroke in that home while sitting in her chair watching her favorite TV daytime show, *General Hospital.* She passed away in the hospital.

My grandfather would remain in that house until age 96. At times, he would be found on top of the roof fixing a shingle (reported by a neighbor). He would refuse visitors at the door. He would grow bitter and lonely. Eventually, he would be moved into a nursing home.

He passed at the age of 103 from natural causes. He was very friendly when we visited him in the nursing home. He would always ask about his house. We would lie and tell him it was just fine. He was a very dedicated husband to my grandmother. They both lived a good life together.

THE VISIT. I must have been around the age of 35 (my grandfather was still living in the nursing home) when we (children) were allowed inside the house to look around at its current state of condition. I recall my nervousness entering the home (alone) but felt more confident as an adult than as a child-teen being there. After all, I should have grown out of that stage of nervousness by now ... right? Guess not. Does one ever forget what set the foundation of scary for them at a young age?

In that house, the foundation for me was how I could not seem to get past my explanation of why I was having physical and emotional reactions in my being there.

As I walked through the front door (alone), the feelings I had once felt as a child-teen began to resurface in my mind with every step I took. The mission of my visit that day was to go upstairs and view what had been left in boxes. I did not spend much time looking around inside the house. I felt like I was being watched no matter where I stood. As I approached the stairs, I looked up toward the closed curtain. Taking a deep breath, I made my way up each step feeling more uptight as I reached the top. The emotions I had felt as a child-teen were **triggered** by my memories being there alone. I recall telling myself that I had nothing to fear. That fear soon fell on deaf ears.

TOP OF STAIRS. As I grabbed the curtain and pushed it aside, it would take me a few minutes to calm my nerves to acclimate to the conditions around me. The smell of the musky curtain was as strong as ever with dust falling off it. My first and only stop would be the PINK bedroom (to the right) to view a few boxes of memorabilia.

As I walked into the PINK room, the air felt light but had a hint of an old-aged wood scent. The original bed I had slept on as a child (one or two times) remained in the room. The room appeared smaller than I had once remembered. Sitting on the edge of the bed, I grabbed my first box to look at memorabilia. *What I did not know at the time was "something" was in that room watching my every move ... ready to make its own ... "on me."*

ATTACKED. As I began to glance at each item in the box, it was no more than ten minutes when I began feeling sick to my stomach. Symptoms that came on suddenly were a mild headache, feeling dizzy, fuzzy thinking (like my head was in a drum), and stomach pains. These symptoms were puzzling to me feeling because I had felt fine entering the home. I was now experiencing illness. It was also at this point that the room conditions changed (from light air to heavy air). My breathing began to labor. I reminded myself there was nothing to fear thinking I was triggering my mind into having a panic attack.

I was probably in that room no more than fifteen minutes when I felt the air getting heavier and an intense smell of something rotten (sulfur) or decomposing (deceased animal) drifting around me. I looked toward the wall thinking a mouse may have died in it. I noticed the burnt curtain. It is believed a recent lightning strike hitting the house may have caused the curtain fire. "Something" put that fire out.

I got up from the bed and attempted to locate the rotten smell. Having a sensitive nose, I would have noticed this rotting dead smell immediately upon my entrance into the room. In fact, the rotting dead smell continued to **intensify** the longer I stayed in the room. Not finding the source, I sat back down and continued to look at memorabilia. It would not be long until I would find myself putting my hands over my nose to not breathe in the horrid smell. Finally, there came a point where I could not stand it anymore and left running down the stairs and OUT of the house.

WHAT JUST HAPPENED TO ME? You may ask if I may have been experiencing a chemical or toxic smell that went unnoticed until I became adjusted to the environment? I am not sure. I know sitting houses have their smells, especially 100-year old houses. Dead mice smell badly but would have been noticed upon my entrance into the room.

Were my headache and dizziness caused by unseen molds or toxins? I did not get the impression there was a mold problem in the house. I am convinced I was **attacked** by "something" negative who just wanted me out of that house.

Feeling good when I went into it and leaving feeling incredibly ill makes me wonder about what was lurking from behind the curtain. The question is, as you read this, is "SOMETHING" still there?

<u>QUESTIONS – THOUGHTS - AFTERMATH</u>

Do I believe I was the target of something negative in that house? Yes. Do I believe it was the former owner (woman) who died in the kitchen-porch fire? Yes. How do I know this? I cannot give you a definite on this, but I am working off a gut feeling.

NEW OWNERS. Two different owners have lived in the home since the departure of my grandparent's. The first owner started renovations but ran out of money. He left. Soon after, with the home sitting empty, a tornado battered it (see page 39).

The second owner, current, turned the place into a junk yard. No discussion has ever been made with either owner about unusual experiences.

QUESTION/THOUGHTS

The question remains ... did my other family members experience unexplained uneasiness in that house? Yes. At what age did others in my family notice? Around the ages of 4 to 8. Did my mother who lived in that house as an older teen (short period of time) ever notice anything? No. Does she feel that house was ever haunted? No.

It is interesting to note when we rented the home as contract for deed to a tenant, as he was working on restructuring the floor plan, a 50-cent coin fell out of the rafters. It dated back to the late 1800's.

It was not uncommon "back in the day" when homes were constructed that owners would board up items in their walls (shoe, picture, bottle, doll, etc.) as their mark and symbol of letting the finder know their presence remained there.

The value of this coin was around $50.00. In the owner's efforts to remodel, he ran out of money and moved. The next owner, a family with young children, purchased the home continuing the effort.

We know how their story is to date ... the place is a mess (outside disaster; can only imagine the inside). A home once in good shape and always tidy ... now a mess.

OTHER ENCOUNTERS IN HOME

THE ESTATE PICKING. Post PINK room experience, I vowed I would never to go inside that house again. The next time I would enter my grandparent's home would be during an estate picking with my family. As a side note, I have always been apprehensive about acquiring items from auctions or estates due to attachments to objects.

During the estate picking, I did not go upstairs to the PINK room. While item picking, two unexplained incidents occurred with one happening to my younger sister, who is also sensitive, and the other incident, to me. To be discussed after you read "definitions."

DEFINITIONS

Agent – a living person who is the focus of poltergeist activity. **Poltergeist** – non-human entity (noisy ghost) usually more malicious or destructive than ghosts or deceased human beings. May involve thumping, banging, levitation or movement of objects, stone throwing, and starting fires. **Intuition** – perceptive insight ("gut feeling"). **Synchronicity** – numerous unrelated variables joining to create a common event or coincidence.

THE MUSIC BOX. During the estate picking, two incidents occurred that involved a **synchronization** of a music box and teeth jar (story follows). A music box was lying on my grandparent's bed. How it got placed onto the bed remains unknown. Tables had been set up in the livingroom displaying our grandparent's possessions for viewing.

My sister recalled she was looking at stuff on a table when she overheard a music box playing. She followed the sound to an adjacent room on the first floor which led her into our grandparent's bedroom. The music box (playing) intrigued her enough to pick it up to inspect it. The pin, which is typically pulled out after winding to make the music box play, remained in a locked position (it should not have played). Startled by this observation, she put it down onto the bed and came and told me about it while I was looking at items on tables.

As I went into the bedroom to investigate, the music box had stopped playing. No surprise there.

THE TEETH JAR. Thinking my sister was imagining things with that music box turned my attention to a table in front of me that had a jar with a mix of several baby teeth in it. It just so happens my grandparents saved our baby teeth they had pulled (my siblings and cousins) displaying them in a jar they placed in their cupboard.

Side Note: My grandfather prided himself in his teeth pulling methods such as using a string attached to a door, a wrench the size of a fist, and all other types of tooth extraction methods. You would think the fear of him using those methods alone would make the tooth fall out on its own.

I recall no one touching anything on any of the tables during the viewing session. I also remember the room was still with no chaotic movement or vibration causing items to topple over on their own. In fact, all items on the tables sat secured in their positions. I was puzzled when I spotted a jar half full of baby teeth. What I should not have done was make a snide comment about it ... "why would anyone collect and store teeth in a jar?" As others were distracted looking elsewhere, it was at the point of my comment that a jar "jumped" toward me falling on top of other items. This no doubt startled me.

Everyone heard something fall and looked in my direction. I explained I had nothing do with the jar falling but told them it jumped out at me on its own. They looked at me with blank stares and in disbelief. After all, jars don't jump.

QUESTIONS / THOUGHTS

Could these moments have been a **synchronization** of paranormal activity? The music box and the teeth jar?

Was "something" present? Or were these moments just pure coincidence? How many coincidences must occur before **intuition** is tossed to the wind? Music boxes do not play in a shut off mode positions, or do they? Teeth jars do not jump at someone when solidly positioned on a table, or do they? As I look back on these situations, it is apparent to me that something was trying to get our [or my] attention. I do not believe it was the spirit of my grandmother. My grandfather was still alive and in the nursing home. I believe it was the "unseen" upstairs.

SIDE NOTE. When the teeth jar jumped out at me, I did make a comment to all in the room that no more remarks should be made about our grandparent's possessions. A belief I have about the afterlife is that they can still hear us. To this day, I also do not make fun of objects picked at auctions, estate sales, or garage sales. I have since experienced other "jumping objects" in my husband's presence with no conclusive explanation other than most incidents seem to occur during a new or full moon phase.

CURTAIN FIRE. Is it possible for ghosts to protect the homes in which they had once lived or feel comfortable in? I speculate the answer to this question might be, "maybe." Although I cannot offer evidence or proof of my opinion, there have been some interesting weather events that should have caused damage to my grandparent's house to the point of its full destruction.

LIGHTNING STRIKE. My grandparent's home was hit by a lightning strike shortly after my grandfather was moved into a nursing home. The lightning strike caused the curtain on the second floor (PINK room) to start on fire. This is the same room I felt I was attacked in. Although this curtain should have blazed into flames, it was as if something had patted it out leaving singed edges. Coincidence? Maybe. Could it be possible that the material it was made was flame retardant? Doubtful. Recall, this house had a fire in the kitchen causing the death of a woman years before my grandparent's took possession of it. Could the curtain fire been put out by "something" wanting to protect its comfortable home? I say anything is possible. I am leaning toward "yes."

TORNADO. It was within a year or two after the curtain fire incident when a F4 tornado would hit the town (grandfather still in nursing home) causing widespread damage to many homes. Many of the homes near and next to my grandparent's house had to be torn down. My grandparent's house stood and still stands as one of "the oldest" homes in that town.

Damage to my grandparent's home included all windows being broken, a board pierced through the wall from the outside into the kitchen, police radio found in the middle of the dining room floor along with a bunch of money (paper, not coins) next to it. See image page 39.

QUESTIONS/THOUGHTS

Was destruction of the home spared by the unpredictable wind currents of the storm? Or was there "something" in the home that offered its assistance in protecting it?

These questions may never get answered. I have always been fascinated by the bizarre effects of weather. Hearing a piece of straw pierced a tree (right through its trunk) ... almost like threading a needle. Vehicles ending up in other people's garages perfectly parked and untouched. Houses lifted from their foundation and found in the backyards on other people's properties. It is no wonder something as odd as finding a police radio along with money in the middle of a dining room floor should not be as surprising as it sounds. Old Spice (grandfather) and perfume/talcum powder (grandmother) smells embedded in the bathroom cabinet remain as memory scents.

FAST FORWARD 2021

See pictures on page 39. First image ... house ravaged by tornado. Bottom image, house looks tired even after acquiring new siding. One of few oldest houses in town.

Arrow on the left, points down where the kitchen fire took place killing female owner. Arrow upper right top, where I believe negative entity hung out (not PINK room). Bottom arrow, sunroom where I sat for hours to avoid going into the house. Has "something" moved on after two new owners? No idea.

<u>Once A House of Love</u>
Tenant After Grandparents … He Left

Tornado Aftermath

Current Owner … Disaster Backyard

Chapter 3
Psychic Warns of Powerful Mind

Illustration by Brandy Woods

Chapter 3
Psychic Warns of Powerful Mind

MY STORY

Post-flood (my age 4), my family left the "pewee house" and purchased a single-family home (basement house) five miles outside of town that resided on higher ground. It would be on this property (ages 4-18) that new chapters would be introduced into my life.

Around my age of 5, during a heavy rain, our basement house flooded (old foundation). It was in the early morning hours when I would be awakened by my mother saying, "we need to get out of here." As I waded through inches of water (ankle high) in my pajamas in cold water, all I could think about was my getting electrocuted. Most kids do not think like this at this age.

Walking through inches of flood water ankle high was another sensation I will never forget. Instead of selling the home, my parents decided to build a house on top of the basement house. My father also built a barn out back.

Living life from ages 6 to 18 on this rural property was no picnic for me. Bored out of my mind with little to entertain me, at least my siblings and I were able to play in the woods that resided behind the barn.

41

I spent most of my school years (pre- and post) feeling depressed and isolated. As a rural kid, no kid from town wanted to spend any time with you. As a result, the feeling of isolation set in. To make matters worse, I lived in a turbulent home atmosphere that never ended.

I didn't grow up with alcoholic or drug addict parents. I grew up in the country (rural) with little stimulation to keep me entertained, no focus (presume ADHD), and no parental time to drag me to and from school activities.

Our family persona was known to surrounding neighbors as "perfectly raised" children who never got into any trouble. However, like all families, we remained silent with our troubles. Our portrayal was not as it seemed.

Striving to remain "perfect" was a struggle. Eventually, people would start to react with jealousy or ask questions. Those who were jealous of me would turn my friends against me. Eventually, I would start hearing, "you think you know so much." Hardly. I could barely pass a math class. I pretended I was on top of my game. I began to internalize my pain and anger. I trusted no one.

This was the point where I saw a psychologist (my doing) to help me figure myself out. He offered little help. All he wanted to do was to put me under hypnosis and on anti-depressant medication. My pain and anger worsened. I developed an ulcer from my miserable life.

There came a point when two traumatic events occurred after I vocalized to the universe my pain and hurt from each of the sources. I would tell the universe to do back to others as they had done to me. My specific request was to double their pain. I cannot share with you what I wished for or happened, but the universe responded.

SEEKING OUT PSYCHICS

This was the point I began seeking out psychics. I felt credible psychics would be able to help me understand my world better than a psychologist. I felt they could also foresee and forewarn me of negative situations allowing me an opportunity to try and change their outcomes.

THE PSYCHIC READING

The first psychic I reached out to ended up in jail for being a fraud. What's new – story of my life. Why is it the first one of anything is the worst for me and the ones after are better. This fraud, by the way, ended up on the 6:00 PM news. At the point I told her off, she became angry and told me she would curse me for several years. Reminds me of the "evil eye" woman I had an incident with while in France (I took her picture which she didn't like).

LaJeanne, my next psychic, was not only good, but great. Attitudes about psychics forty years ago was a taboo topic. You never shared with anyone that you went to a psychic because people thought they were a two-bit carnival act and then, they looked at you like you were crazy.

After sharing with LaJeanne the two traumatic incidents that occurred, I asked her if I was responsible for them. She told me "no" (what else was she to say, "yes")? She informed me and impressed upon me that my words and thoughts were powerful due to my internalizing pain and anger. She told me my brain (mind) was unusually powerful and to learn how to control and calm my anger (which I had internalized for years). I had always wondered – why wasn't my mind bringing me positive events? The answer, "I needed to believe in positive."

As a side note, LaJeanne was hired to serve a role with the police department. As a psychic, she attempted to locate missing children.

I learned much from her. She was able to explain to me why people react the way they do toward me. Forty years ago, she predicted my future. I continue to internalize painful situations involving people's actions and words.

DEFINITIONS

Anger – a strong feeling of annoyance, displeasure, or hostility. **High Sensitivity** – physical, acute, mental, and emotional responses to internal or external stimuli. **Mind Intention** – purposeful state of mind accompanying an act; the manipulation to achieve a foreseen unlawful end. **Psychic** – relating to or denoting faculties or phenomena that are apparently inexplicable by natural laws, especially involving telepathy or clairvoyance.

QUESTIONS/THOUGHTS

Is it possible to manifest situations or inflict retaliatory pain on others who have wronged you ... simply by asking the universe to respond? The answer is "yes." But be careful, this can act like a mirror and backfire.

You need to wish for positive outcomes for yourself. Be careful what you "think of" and "wish for."

I Am An Artist. I Love Color. Color Calms Me.
These Lupines Are Lavender.

45

Chapter 4
Faces in the Window Screen
Do You See Us?

Illustration by Kelly Renee Schutz
Filtered to Show Ghost People in Window Screen
Home Burned Down March 7, 2020

REAL IMAGE - NOT FAKE

Chapter 4
Faces in the Window Screen

PHENOMENA

My visits to my paternal grandparent's farm as a child and teen were few. On the rare occasion I stayed overnight, my experience in their country home, built around 1904, would provide me with a snapshot of what life may have been like living in that house in a time when few homes had modern facilities. This home initially had no indoor plumbing or electricity. Eventually, electricity only.

ORIGINAL HOME. Since the passing of my grandfather and grandmother, the house remained empty with no one to care of it. Although the house had fallen into disrepair, what remained were remnants of its original architecture and solid construction. This speaks to the exceptional craftsmanship my great grandfather, a farmer and carpenter, had put into the making of that home. This home would eventually pass to his son and then, to my father. Three, nearly four-five, generations.

WAS SOMEBODY WATCHING ME? As a sensitive teen, my visits to this home made me feel uncomfortable. Not being familiar enough with the property, there were moments when I had convinced myself that evil surrounded it causing me to avoid the place entirely. I cannot explain why I felt this way. I always blamed that feeling on the way the house looked even though the home was the most "grand structure" of its time and in the county.

GENEAOLOGY. When I was in my early 30's, I made a visit to see my grandmother to discuss the family genealogy. She showed me a picture of a young girl and boy who stood side by side. These children would be the brother (Andrew) and sister (Mary) of my grandfather. Mary passed away around the age of 9-10 years old in my great grandfather's "first home" approximately 2 miles down the road. Andrew lived a full life. Although the young gal in the window screen appears to be Mary, what is interesting to me is that she looks to be 6-7 years old. She has the shape of face and smile as her parents. Her hair appears to be pulled down and back around her head though this was a common hairstyle then. See image that follows. What is also confusing is the man who stands above her. In review of many pictures I have of my great grandfather, what creates confusion is that it appears he did not sport a mustache. The man in the window screen appears to have a mustache. The only other explanation is that the illusion is a deep shadow around his lips. Who is this man?

In seeking the help from an expert psychic, this man is either my great grandfather or is the doctor who cared for Mary on her death bed. I have struggled to verify the identity of this man. See image that follows.

Real Images (Not Fake)
Man and Little Girl
May 6, 2007

Photo by Kelly Renee Schutz
Do You See Us Now?

49

DEFINITIONS

Earthbound – a ghost or spirit unable to cross over to the other side at the time of death and is therefore stuck on earth. **Ghost** – a ghost is believed to be the soul or the life force of a person or animal. **Ghost Hunter** – a person who attempts to gather information of paranormal activity. **Materialization –** the formation of a visible physical form of a spirit. **Matrixing – w**hen the mind attempts to manifest images of something they are not. **Manifestation** – the appearance or taking of form of an entity. **Skeptic** – to question what others may perceive as real or true.

MY ENCOUNTER

My grandmother passed away a couple of months prior to my taking the picture as seen on the previous page. She left the house vacant and sitting alone. On May 6, 2007, I photographed the ghostly images in the window screen when I made a visit to the property to say goodbye to my grandparents in spirit. It was at this time that I thought this would be my final images and visit to their home. However, little did I realize, I would make several visits back to their home to use my ghost equipment to attempt to make further contact with what showed to me in the window screen or any entity roaming the home and property.

QUESTIONS AND THOUGHTS

Were my suspicions as a teenager confirmed about the property BEING haunted when the images showed in the window? Or did the property BECOME haunted once my grandparents passed leaving the property empty yet triggering ghostly residents to come back to live in their comfortable home? From what I was told by a ghost expert, the house has a portal underneath its foundation and brings into it all sorts of "unwanted" guests.

THE BRAIN GAME

In 2016, I watched a television show called, "*Brain Games*." This show demonstrated how the mind is easily fooled and confused when shown images of people's faces "upside down." Most people viewed these images as "right side up" and formed images in their minds that made the images look "human." Because our minds "see" human faces continually, this is why the brain naturally creates images to look "human-like."

If that is true, then, why is it that when the image was shown to about 200 people that they would all DESCRIBE the image with the EXACT SAME details? Or were their minds playing tricks on them?

YOU BE THE JUDGE. Do you see what appears to be a man, hovering over a young girl in the screened window? Do you see him wearing glasses, his nose, a possible mustache, and his chin? Do you see his eyes? Or is your brain fooling you by putting these details into the picture?

Although one could argue the facial details of the man are what men looked like in the 1900's, one cannot simply deny that what you see is oddly real and described the same way in detail by those who see it.

Brain Game?   Not all people look alike. What makes this man look unique is that you can actually "see" what appears to be his facial details. Same with the little girl. She appears to be smiling. What is certain though – they are both looking right at me.

ABILITY TO MANIFEST

So, what caused these faces to manifest in the window screen? Most ghosts can only hold their image for about 3-5 seconds. Although most ghosts appear at night (due to mistaken reflections, shadows, and stronger energy fields), ghosts can also appear during the daytime.

It just so happens this manifestation came forth due to a straight-line wind that occurred the morning of my arrival ripping through the property. This storm had knocked over a large tree (away from the house) onto a powerline. With so much electricity still resonating in the air from the storm, you could hear the buzzing sound and feel the electromagnetic waves.

It is also believed that a lightning bolt hit the property causing the limestone foundation beneath the home to act as a conductor or absorber for energy. It is also believed these factors combined allowed for the manifestation of the man and young gal in the window.

GHOST HUNTING VISITS CONTINUE

As a paranormal investigator, in order to prove what I photographed in the window that day was real (not mind matrixing), I would need to visit the property several times thereafter to capture more evidence. As a matter of fact, I did capture a moving orb in the basement, a solid orb moving around the livingroom, had my camera batteries die in the barn, and was surrounded by hundreds of orbs when standing on the front steps of the home on a full moon evening. All situations where I captured evidence occurred during a storm or moon phase.

DAY TRIP IN 2017

My sister and I always liked to ghost hunt on the property (house and barn). There was a day (afternoon) mid-2017 (cannot recall if March or later), when we decided to go to the property to ghost hunt. With the house falling apart and black mold taking over the kitchen ceiling, it was important to bring masks to not breathe in black mold spreading all over the house. Our intent was to not stay in the house very long. Of course, we forgot to bring masks.

Battling tall weeds and grass to get to the falling apart house was always a challenge. During the earlier months, several wood ticks would cling to a person just walking a short path to the front door of the house. This was one way to keep unwanted visitors from going over there.

As we approached the house, we noticed the hole (outside porch leading into the house) was getting bigger. This small area was just enough to detain a person from entering with ease. A risk for anyone who didn't understand that stepping into that hole would result in falling 5' feet downward onto a dirt covered basement while cutting up their legs (rotting wood).

As we entered the door that led into the kitchen, my sister and I noticed the black mold on the ceiling spreading. It looked as if its mission were to take over the entire place.

 I do not believe we went upstairs that day although it was in as bad as shape as the downstairs. The narrow steps that led upstairs were always covered with white dry wall pieces ... making the journey to reach the top even more difficult and risky.

The house and property had no electricity. It did have, though, copper wiring in its walls. The rooms (diningroom, livingroom, adjacent porch, and upstairs) were all rotting from the inside out.

The pink (or were they green) curtains still hung in their places (diningroom and livingroom) as if they were forgotten. A small candle, never burned, still sat on the ledge in a window in the livingroom. Cannot recall if the pink hand-held dial phone on the wall remained.

Mice that didn't survive the winter lie flattened (decomposed) on the diningroom floor among a lot of ceiling tile debris and insulation. The walls in the livingroom, covered with a wet runny mold stain from top to bottom, remind us that deterioration occurs over time.

The sewing area (a nook) was completely rotted out. The narrow porch, attached to the home, was falling off. The place was and still is, as of this writing, a deterioration mess. Despite all of this, the ghosts do not seem to mind the look of the deteriorated environment and gather there for whatever reason.

With K-2 meter in hand (sweatshirts over our noses), my sister and I proceeded to walk into the kitchen area. As we stood and stared at its condition, we began visualizing how it was set up back in the day. After all, two, nearly three-four generations lived in this house.

It would later be discovered that much of the furniture that remained in that house was handed down from my great grandfather to grandfather to father. Much of it now in the hands of my generation, the great grandchildren.

As my sister and I stood in the kitchen, we began asking questions to attempt to make contact. Regardless of the moon phase that day (clear afternoon), we were successful. But with "whom" did we make contact?

The house and barn seem to be haunted every time we go over there. My ghost application device spit out the words "UPON ... EVERYONE." I took that to mean that we stumbled upon a group gathering. Distracted for just a second, as we looked away, my K-2 meter then zipped to 5 bubbles (we saw it). It was at this point that I felt breathless and needed to get out of the house. I did not know if it was because I was being affected by the black mold or the lack of oxygen while breathing underneath my sweatshirt.

As we were leaving, I felt like I was going to pass out. My sister walked ahead of me. I instructed her to keep an eye on me because I could not breathe very well. The sense I had was that something was wrapped around me. I then felt attachments all over me. But who was attaching? And of course ... why?

As I entered my car, I kept shaking myself in all directions telling whomever to get off me and go back to the house. As I turned the car on, I needed to continue my plea with a stern voice. The feeling of having something attached to me subsided about a mile down the road.

At the point my father passed away in December 2016, I was not able to go back inside this house alone. However, I would sit in my car at the end of the driveway and look at a property that was once in its glory days ... a beauty of the county ... now a deteriorated mess. Let me not forget to mention ... also a property haunted by not one, but many ghosts (former residents and strangers).

Beloved Home Built 1901 Burned Down March 7, 2020 by New Owner of Property

Tales of Apparitions #1

Chapter 5
The Tree Swing

Photo Illustration by Kelly Renee Schutz
Tales of Apparitions

Chapter 5
The Tree Swing

"Stay off of that tree swing," I said to my 12-year old niece. "Why can't I sit on it?" she says. "Because it is only for decoration and is not safe to sit on or ride. You could hurt yourself," I replied. "I sat on it yesterday and nothing happened," niece replies. "Stay off of it, please," I said.

My not wanting my niece to sit on the tree swing didn't have anything to do with it directly. I knew the tree limb was strong enough to hold her weight and knew the swing functioned properly. However, what I struggled with was telling her that on occasion, I would look outside my kitchen window on a calm day and actually see the swing moving "back and forth" ... "back and forth" ... "higher and higher," as if someone were pushing it.

I recall the first time I noticed the tree swing moving like this. I just froze in place and stared directly at it. Most of the time, I would shake this off as being my imagination, I blamed it on how the wind caught it. However, it was when it looked like someone grabbed the seat and stopped it that I thought otherwise.

About forty years ago, long before this property became part of my subdivision, the land belonged to a farmer, his wife, and three children (Alicia, Samantha, and Frank). The father built his home, now torn down due to subdivision regulations, and cleared a small backyard for his small children to play in. Back then, I suppose you could say his property looked like all the rest ... modern for its time and comfortably lived in.

Having a hand in carpentry, the father constructed for his children, a playground consisting of a wooden swing set with three swings, teeter-totter, and merry-go-round. I would imagine the kids felt as if they had it all and were the envy of the neighbor kids.

One day, the three children went outside to play while the parents worked steadily on chores around the farm. Alicia and Samantha, two of the youngest siblings, had told their older brother, Frank, to push them on the swing set. As Frank took turns going from one to the other, pushing Alicia and then pushing Samantha, each became overly excited telling him to push them "higher and higher." The girls soared like birds.

As excitement and laughter roared in the air from each of the girls, Frank tirelessly rushed from one to the other to see how high he could push each of them. Eventually, there came a point when the wooden swing set structure could not support the amount of pressure it was given and collapsed. Alicia was thrown forward in the air finding herself hitting the ground hard. Samantha was thrown backwards, losing her balance, and hitting her head on a large rock that was positioned behind the set. Both girls lied motionless on the ground with blood coming out of their noses and mouths. Frank was horrified from the sight.

Frank ran to get his mother for help. As the mother and father returned, it was obvious that both girls could not be revived and both perished onsite from their injuries. When the mother asked Frank what had happened, Frank told her they were *just* swinging and the structure suddenly collapsed. The mother blamed the father for the death of the young girls due to poor construction of the swing set.

Illustration by Brandy Woods

What remained on the property when we purchased their home was the wooden teeter-totter the father built for the kids. The teeter-totter sat motionless in its original place. On occasion, the mother of the deceased girls would look out her kitchen window and imagine it moving "up and down" as if the two girls were playing on it.

A few years had passed. The mother, grief stricken, was committed to and died in a state hospital. The father, feeling isolated and lonely, died from alcoholism. Frank, the brother of the two girls, committed suicide taking his secret about what really happened that day to his grave.

Flash forward. When I look outside and notice the tree swing moving, I can see a rhythm to it as if it were being pushed by someone. There are moments when I can actually hear faint laughter and singing, "la-lah-la-lah-la-lah." You can almost see Frank running back and forth from one to the other girl to see how "high" he could push each of them. "Higher, Frank ... higher!"

GHOST CHILDREN

Living children, especially under the age of 9 years old, can attract the ghosts of children to them. At this age, most children are open and can sense the feelings of others. Adults have a tendency to grow cold and block the world from their vision and emotions. Depending on the age, some children can interact with and visually see ghost children and adults. Although I have not heard of cases where ghost children purposefully seek to harm a living child, many may want to **encourage** a living child to do as they once did -- jump off a building, climb a tree, or swim in a river. Some of these entities could be tricksters.

Photo Illustration by Kelly Renee Schutz
Consent Given for Image

Chapter 6
Poltergeist

Illustration by Halida Dwi Edyati

Chapter 6
Poltergeist

HISTORY OF LAND

This chapter has been updated. In speaking to one of my neighbors, who has encountered unusual activity in their home, it has become apparent to me that we are experiencing different types of phenomena.

In her research, back in the day, a farmer and his family use to reside on both of our parcels of land. This farmer, according to her research, was always disgruntled about something and use to beat (assault, hurt) his wife and children. Angry man. We all know that imprints of negativity can be left behind before and after death.

In comparing her experiences in her home to that of my own, something appears not to be the same with the types of disturbances. Keep in mind, my neighbor has two pre-teen/teen children and two active (large) house dogs, and a husband [which can change what we experience].

Knowing we live in a county riddled with disturbances of the past (Indian uprising) or personal unrest (farmer) ... maybe we can add to our properties two more disturbances ... rattling (vibration) of a train passing through each day **and** what use to be, the MN Dragway.

HISTORY OF MINNESOTA DRAGWAYS

Smoke. Squealing tires. Roars of spectators. Stunt performers. Loud action. Disturbed ground. Welcome to the Minnesota Dragways.

From 1959 until 1976, a stretch of flat land in Coon Rapids, Minnesota was the site of the popular Minnesota Dragways. Its speedway attracted local racers and top pros from around the country who tested their skills and machines in a quarter mile. After the raceway closed, the land sat idle until it was developed into a housing division.

Guess where I live today? Yes, indeed. We live on what use to be a part of the Minnesota Dragways.

We speculate our home was built near the staging area and tower. I always comment to people that our house probably sits on the porta potty area.

The finish line, not too far from our house, is marked by an entrance to our county's compost site. On a Saturday or Sunday afternoon, back in the day, local racers would warm up the crowd facing off as they drove their pride and joys (cars) down the main drag.

Although fans preferred to stand along a chain-link fence near the finish line to watch the racers open their parachutes slowing their vehicles to a stop ... hundreds stood from one end to the other.

Famous names, such as Don "The Snake" Prudhomme and Tom "Mongoose" McEwen were in the drag line-up. Perhaps the most famous, Evel Knievel, would draw the biggest crowd showing off his death defying stunts. In July 1972, he would jump three vans and eight cars in his steam-powered Harley Davidson. Impressive.

LIVING ON A PORTA POTTY

When we moved into our house, we had no idea we would be living on pieces of history. Or as I speculate as of late, disturbed land.

One cannot just isolate the unusual occurrences in a couple of our homes in my neighborhood on the Minnesota Dragway.

Fifty years of loud racing and bouncing on a road strip has a way of imprinting itself into an environment. True. So does a rattling (vibrations) train, a farmer, and an Indian uprising. Just put these thoughts into your pocket for now.

WHERE WE CAME FROM

We moved from two haunted homes from a central midwestern state to a similar aged home in the upper Midwest. A change in our environment would bring us to one that had also experienced a drastic change.

We thought to ourselves ... "this time, we will get some peace from ghosts." Or would we?

PHENOMENA

DOOR LOCKED. You meet with your painter outside to discuss painting portions of the house. As you attempt to go back into the house, you find you are locked out. As you try to go inside through the garage, you find this door is also locked. No one has been inside the house but you.

SCRATCHES. You had surgery and your caretaker is at your home watching over you. She hears sounds in the house and goes to investigate. Scratches are coming from inside a violin case that belonged to your great grandfather. It was sitting on top of a washstand in the washer/dryer room. She looks inside the case.

FLASHES OF LIGHT. Moments later, she sees a flash of light shoot straight up and down in your livingroom. She then hears scratches in the livingroom and behind your head in the room where you are sleeping. She senses something paranormal is in your house. You assure her you are not afraid of unseen forces.

CUPS. You are in the bathroom, which is located next to the washer/dryer room. You hear a loud bang in the kitchen pantry. The kitchen pantry is on the other side of the washer/dryer room. You open the pantry door to discover the plastic cups package (that was on the top shelf) is now on the floor positioned without damage. They had launched off the top shelf hitting against the door. You think to yourself, "I had a feeling something was in here."

RESISTANCE. You are sleeping soundly in a room off the main floor when your husband wakes you up and says, "you will never guess what just happened to me." You ask, "what?" He says, "something was holding the door back as I was coming in from the garage" … "whatever it was, wouldn't let me into the house." "I had to push the door with force to get in." The door leading into the house from the garage goes directly into the washer/dryer room and was unobstructed. It is an easy door to push open.

WARDROBE DOOR. You and your husband are going out to dinner. As you walk into the garage from the washer/dryer room, you notice the 1926 wardrobe (estate pick belonging to great grandfather) door had flung wide open. For the past eight months, the door to the wardrobe was swollen shut and could not be opened without a pick or screwdriver to pull the keyhole. You scream in disbelief.

FALL #1. You are walking down the stairs from the upper level. Without notice, something smooth glides under your feet causing you to fall down the steps spraining your toe.

FALL #2. On another day, you are walking down the stairs to the basement. As you warn your husband to be careful (bringing boxes down), something glides under your feet again and causes you to tumble down injuring your back.

KNOCKING. You are sleeping in bed when you are awakened by the sound of "knocking" (two knocks) near your right side. The last time you heard knocks like this was in Las Vegas when you believe you had an alien visitation. You slowly open your eyes and see nothing. You turn over and pull the covers over your head.

CIGARETTE. You smell a light cigarette scent in your office nightly. Neither of you smoke. In reviewing footage from your night vision camera, a solid orb flies rapidly around your office after you leave and turn out the lights.

SHOVEL. You and your husband are eating dinner around 7:30 PM. You both hear sounds of a shovel scraping against a sidewalk. You comment, "why would the neighbor boy being shoveling our sidewalk now?" You go to the door to see who is outside. No one. A month or so later, you are awakened around 3:00-3:30 AM to hear the exact same sound (shovel scraping against the sidewalk). Except this time, the sound is coming from inside your bedroom. No one is outside shoveling. No train is in the area. Bizarre incident.

INTERCOM. You are sleeping in your TV room. Your husband is watching sports. Without notice, your wireless intercom in that room is screaming out white noise. You wake up. You hear someone trying to mumble a word or two. No other intercom went off except that one. A week or so later, you are downstairs when the intercom in your office goes off. Same thing. Your husband's intercom nor the ones downstairs went off. What is happening?

DOOR OPEN-CLOSE. You are working in your office late one evening (1:00 AM). You hear the front door open and close. You think it is your husband looking outside. Moments later, your husband walks down to your office (from a dead sleep) and says to you, "did the front door just open and close?" You both look at each other with fear in your eyes. You investigate the entire house. Nothing to be found. Deadbolt is latched. Say what?

DEFINITIONS

Agent – a living person who is the focus of poltergeist activity. **Apparition** – an unusual or unexpected sight or situation; materialization just after manifestation. **Authentication** – proving genuine verification of facts surrounding an occurrence of paranormal phenomena. **Chance** – random, unpredictable influences on events. **Clairaudience** – auditory form of ESP paranormal information received outside the range of normal perception through voices, whispers, and auditory impressions. **Intuition** – perceptive insight ("gut feeling"). **Imprint** – a sound heard with no explanation; happens without warning. **Intelligent Haunting** – an interaction on the physical plane as in communication or object movement from a spirit who is conscious. **Place-Centered Haunting** – a location where paranormal events frequently take place. **Poltergeist** – non-human entity (noisy ghost) usually more malicious or destructive than ghosts or deceased human beings. May involve thumping, banging, levitation or movement of objects, stone throwing and starting fires. **Portal** – a location where spirits or entities enter the physical realm. **Psychokinesis –** the ability to move objects by mental effort alone **Residual –** movement or touch that repeats itself in the same manner without warning, not necessarily a viewable event. **Synchronicity** – numerous unrelated variables joining to create a common event or coincidence.

QUICK ANALYSIS

DISTURBED LAND. My husband and I thought House #4 would be different. Wrong. Seems like we are always sharing space with ghost occupants. I suppose they (the ghosts) would say the same.

After departing from House #3, I swore I would lay off ghost hunting for a few years. I wanted a less bothered life. Our move to Minnesota into a 16-year old house situated on a former motor dragway would prove to be more of the same. Disturbed land? Maybe.

Ghosts seem enjoy my company. They follow me everywhere. If they do exist in a home, they make me believe I am their "trigger object." According to my dentist, I live in an area that is haunted. After all, the Halloween capital of the world is right down the road from us.

No one seems to know WHY this area is haunted. Not only do we have presumed residual imprints from a former loud energy filled motor dragway but my home is also on land where the Chippewa and Sioux Indians battled another for territorial rights.

Disturbed land? Maybe. If anything, "FULL" of energy.

LOCKED OUT. It just so happens, the day I was locked out of the house during my painting renovation discussion, was a day I was on strong medication making me physically ill every 30 minutes. No laughing matter to me. However, to the ghost … no mercy and probably enjoyed every minute of my pain.

I only stepped out of the house for a few minutes. How could I have been locked out? With no one in the house, the next quest was to figure out HOW the deadbolt got into a locked position. Something had to shut the door and turn the lock. Otherwise, the deadbolt would have set itself against the door frame.

It was at this point I knew we had a ghost … yes, an uninvited guest. Or was this "thing" an occupant?

WARNING. I would never advise you to turn on your apps or K2 meters in your homes. These devices act like a Ouija board drawing in unwanted entities. Entities you may have a difficult time getting rid of.

GHOST APP – CONVERSATION WITH JOHN. In my wanting to get down to "who" had just locked me out of the house, once the painter left, I pulled out my ghost app and started asking questions. This ghost app relays words. I have used this app many times understanding intelligent responses and random non-sense.

Caution #1: As mentioned previously, never play with ghost hunting instruments in your own house. They act like Ouija boards (potentially bringing in more unwanted spirits).

Caution #2: Ghost apps are not always reliable. Words expressed could be random. For "entertainment" purposes only. Know your equipment.

QUESTION AND RESPONSE

When I asked the ghost app who was in the house and who had just locked me out ... the response I received came quickly ... "John." Okay, who is John?

Three years later (as of this writing), I believe I may have found out the answer. In a recent discussion with one of my neighbors, I learned a parent passed away in one of the homes. It just so happens the son's name (who owns the home) is Jonathan.

Was this the ghost of our neighbor's parent trying to reach out to him? I remain on the fence. Inconclusive.

Caution #3: If you believe you have identified the ghost by name, do not call its name out loud or bring attention to it. What you may be doing is manifesting something stronger. Most importantly, never trust it is a "nice" ghost.

HUSBAND FORCING DOOR OPEN. Time had passed by since the door locking incident. That was until my caretaker (post-surgery) came over to babysit me.

What I learned from having a stranger in my home is that they too can bring unwanted ghosts in or trigger situations. Once the caretaker left, the poltergeist activity began in full force. For one to one and a half weeks.

The first noticeable incident was when I was sleeping in a room off the main floor. My husband was working in the garage when he decided to call it a day.

As he attempted to open the door leading into the house from the garage (which, by the way, led into the washer/dryer room), he found himself not being able to move the door more than SIX inches.

At first, he was in disbelief that he could not open the door. It was as if something was standing behind holding it back. He then pulled the door toward him and pushed it hard into the room. I would bet whatever was holding him back went flying into the wall.

Husband wakes me up from my sleep to tell me what happened. It takes a lot of strength for a ghost to hold a door firmly (to the point of needing force to open it).

KITCHEN PANTRY. Sometimes, I wonder, did the force of him shoving that door open cause a delayed energetic reaction?

A few days after his "can't get the door open" incident, I was using the bathroom when I heard a loud, "THUMP." I thought, "what was that?" It sounded as if it came from the kitchen. In my investigation, I opened the pantry door and discovered the plastic cups (packaged) lying on the floor in an upright position. Prior to this happening, they were on the top shelf in a secured position. Ghost, lei line, or delayed energetic reaction?

WARDROBE FLINGS OPEN. I purchased my great grandfather's wardrobe (1926) at my father's estate auction in 2018.

Because of its deterioration and repulsive barn smell inside, I set it out in our garage and left it air out for eight months. My husband had intentions to refinish it.

The one obvious issue with this wardrobe, outside of its smell condition, was that the front doors were swollen shut. There was no possible way anyone could open the doors without taking a pick or screwdriver and pulling the keyhole toward them.   76

One evening, my husband and I decided to go out to eat. This incident occurred the very same week as all the other poltergeist situations.

As I walked around the car to get in ... I noticed nothing different about the wardrobe. As I was getting into the driver's side of the car, the minute I opened and closed my door, I looked out my window and noticed the right side of the wardrobe door had flung wide open angled back (further than pictured). Left door remained closed.

If anyone can explain to me how this door opened seconds after I crawled into our vehicle ... I am all ears. The way it swung open gave the appearance that something needed to use the restroom in a hurry. What just happened here? I screamed. Door was swollen shut.

CARETAKER HEARING SCRATCHES. When you meet people for the very first time, you keep a distance. This is a typical, natural, instinct.

One afternoon, as I was sleeping, my caretaker reported to me that she heard scratching. Not having any animals and not being aware of a rodent issue in our walls, she went throughout the house to investigate. She heard scratches coming from the washer/dryer room.

She isolated the noise to my great grandfather's violin case (homemade) (located in the washer/dryer room). No one was aware if he ever played it or received it as a gift. Regardless, I do not know "how attached" he was to it. I purchased it from my dad's estate sale.

From there, she followed the scratching sound into the livingroom. As she was about to sit down in a chair, she saw a flash of light radiate up from the floor to the ceiling and down. Coincidentally, this would be the same spot I noticed moving orbs in the basement go up as they entered the ceiling. She had also seen a flash of light in the foyer area.

PORTAL IN CLOSET-OUIJA BOARD. A week had passed since the caretaker left. All the drama appeared to be calming down. About a month later, I would have a couple of psychics come into the home to give me their impressions. They never heard scratching but pointed out to me that they felt the previous owner (kids) played with a Ouija board in the house. They attempted to close the portal they felt resided in the foyer closet. They also pointed out to me that the bed in the lower basement may have had someone pass away on it. I suspect it was one of my great grandparents or children.

TRIPPED DOWN THE STAIRS. Just about the time I thought the house was back to normal, something decides to send me a personal message. That message was gliding under my feet while I was walking down two sets of stairs.

The first time was upper level to main level. Out of nowhere, I felt my feet lift and down I want. I sprained my toe.

The second time, I was heading down to the basement with a box in my hands and without warning, fell in the same manner. I was just telling my husband to be careful and watch his step. I also felt something glide in the same manner under my feet. A feeling I know so well as I have been touched by ghosts many times. This time, I injured my back.

When I had fallen down the stairs the second time, I knew these situations were not isolated. In fact, I knew, "my friend", the unwanted house guest was still hanging around. Did you say your name is, "John?"

KNOCK, KNOCK: I woke up one night in a sweat after I heard two knocks to my right side. I sleep on the left side of the bed. In reviewing the night vision camera, it appears orb activity is active in that corner. The knocks reminded me of the time I was in Las Vegas, in a popular hotel, by myself. I was lying in bed and two knocks were heard in the wall behind my head. The knocks were identical. It was in the Las Vegas room where I believe I had my first alien visitation.

CIGARETTE SMELL. The previous owners smoked in the house. However, I suspect they smoked in the basement bathroom. When you move into a home, the first thing you do is figure out how to rid smoke that lodges into and emits from your walls. For this reason, I had all the walls painted. Three times in the bathroom in the basement.

Maybe this is what upset "John." Change. After all, any renovation effort shakes up the apple cart. To date, I smell light cigarette smoke around me while working in my office. On rare occasions, when I smell smoke, I will playback our night vision video camera to observe one or two solid orbs flying around.

SHOVEL SCRAPING INSIDE HOUSE. My husband and I have never heard a "shovel scraping the sidewalk" sound in our dining room or bedroom before. Or, I should say, we heard it as clear as a bell when eating ... and ... I heard it as clear as a bell while he was sleeping at 3:00-3:30 AM. How did he not wake up hearing this sound?

Our first experience with this sound occurred while eating dinner. As we were eating, this scraping sound came out of nowhere. We thought, at first, that our neighbor boy was shoveling our sidewalk. Wrong. No one outside. Was it the train that goes through at all times of day shaking the house and hitting its brakes? No. Was it our furnace? No. Was this an imprint of something from the past? Maybe.

There are many unexplained situations that happen in life. This is one of them. I have heard about "imprints" of sounds occurring out of nowhere ... but ... to experience the same sound TWICE ... seems a bit confusing.

What is going on in this house?

INTERCOM (2X).   Ghosts have abilities to communicate through electrical devices. Especially devices that spew white noise. In two separate incidents, our intercoms reacted to "something" sounding off white noise while also mumbling a word. Some have asked if trucker interference may have caused the situations. Doubtful.

In the first incident, as my husband and I were in our TV room (I was sleeping, he was watching sports), out of nowhere, white noise screamed out of the intercom we had in this room (not the others, only this unit). During this incident, we both looked at each other and awaited the intercom to say something. It eventually mumbled a word and stopped. Nothing since.

During the second incident, I was downstairs when my husband heard my intercom go off in my office. Keep in mind, he also has an intercom in his office. Which did not go off. And, where I was, there were two more. He said something was trying to say something on my intercom.

Recall, I smell smoke in my office all the time. Most people believe outside interferences affect electronic devices (scanners, other devices). This does not appear to be the case in either of these situations.

However, with all the poltergeist incidents experienced in our house since Day 1 and with "John" floating around ... something tells me, it was probably, "JOHN."

Yes, outside frequencies can affect wireless devices. We all know this can happen.

WHO OPENED AND CLOSED FRONT FOYER DOOR.
You are working in your office at 1:00 AM. Your office is situated in the furthest part of the house.

The house at 1:00 AM is quiet. No radio, no sounds, no distractions. Without warning, you hear your front door open (casual manner) as if someone were coming in. You then hear it close (same manner). The timing of the opening and closing leads you to believe your husband was looking out the door at something.

What you do not hear as the door opens is the security alarm ring upon entering. You think nothing of this (at first). You wonder to yourself, "why is my husband looking out the door at 1:00 AM?" You go back to work.

A minute later, your husband drags himself down the hallway to your office. As he stands in the doorway, it is obvious to you he just woke up from a dead sleep.

Although the opening-closing was not aggressive, who just came in or left? You decide enough is enough and purchase a night vision video camera to see if you can detect orbs or shadow people in your foyer.

Caution #4. Wireless intercoms and night vision cameras can also attract paranormal activity into your home.

QUESTIONS/THOUGHTS

Are you convinced we have "something" in our house with us? We are. The difficult part about all of this is that we have no clue "who" or "what" it is. My concern is our safety.

Theorists might argue our consciousness may be behind most of our hauntings. I use to defend myself that I couldn't possibly be doing some of this stuff with my mind. However, there are days when I do sit up and wonder.

As of this writing, I know whatever is in here ... is too stubborn to leave. Thankfully, as compared to our previous haunted home situations, it has not attempted to attack or take possession of either of our bodies (yet).

I do not like noticing solid orb activity in our bedroom or my office each night. It makes me wonder what could be so fascinating about floating around in here that it would stay. By the way, what we are seeing is not dust.

I do not speak to "it" to give it attention. I have not used my K2 meter or ghost app for over a year and a half. And, when you bring outsiders into your home (trying to help you), they can bring with them a few more unwanted guests. Just about the time I was giving myself a break ...

Chapter 7
Prince Rupert Hotel–Cycling Mirror

Art Illustration by Brandy Woods
Frightfully True Story As Experienced by Author

Prince Rupert Hotel, Shrewsbury, England

Chapter 7
Prince Rupert Hotel–Cycling Mirror

BRIEF HISTORY

Some historical information about the Prince Rupert Hotel will begin this chapter. A more thorough background can be viewed on the Internet, YouTube, and from a book written by Martin Wood entitled, "Haunted Shrewsbury." The focus of this chapter will be on the reported hauntings at this hotel as well as my own terrifying experience when my husband and I stayed in the Prince Rupert Suite "one" night on May 27, 2016. Would we go back? Only if I were really drunk.

As written in "Haunted Shrewsbury" by Martin Wood, The Prince Rupert Hotel is probably the most haunted hotel in Shrewsbury. The current structure contains parts of homes that range as early as the 1700's. The building dates to approximately the year 1150. Over time, it has experienced the energies of different owners, staff, children, and a variety of personalities.

Named after King Charles I's nephew, Prince Rupert moved to Shrewsbury in 1644 as commander-in-chief of His Majesty's Army and set up his quarters in Jone's Mansion. Jones was an important lawyer in town and the size of his house was testament to his authority.

Mike Matthews, who took over ownership of the hotel in 1996, shares his own haunted experiences on a YouTube video entitled, *Great British Ghosts – The Prince Rupert Hotel, Shrewsbury,* dated September 19, 2012. In this video, he is giving a tour of some of the most haunted rooms to Michaela Strachan, a news reporter, from the Shropshire Star. Together, they walk the hallways, visit rooms, and discuss haunted occurrences. Michaela Strachan is then guided by Martin Wood, local historian, to go down into the cellar where he himself, has been witness to and has had more than one personal haunted experience with an angry gent. See YouTube video link: **https://www.youtube.com/watch?v=TWxN0MYrT3U**

<u>YOUTUBE VIDEO</u>

I was particularly happy to notice that when they filmed this YouTube video clip in 2012, that they went directly into the room where we stayed, "The Prince Rupert Suite." Take a moment to notice the location of the MIRROR. Close to wall by the window.

LOOK WHERE THE MIRROR IS NOW

Look at the image below to see where the MIRROR is positioned when my husband and I stayed in this room on May 27, 2016. It is on the other side of the room, in front of an exit door, right next to the bathroom. You will notice that we propped a luggage rack in front of the bathroom door. It was reported that the door would SLAM shut. I wasn't in the mood for slamming, so we attempted to make the effort more difficult.

However, what we didn't realize was the ghostly entity decided to make its presence known by moving and CYCLING THE MIRROR instead. FULL CYCLE. I can see how difficult it would be to CYCLE itself against the wall/window where it had been originally positioned in 2012.

However, there was plenty of room between it and the exit door to complete a FULL CYCLE during our visit. By the way, we offered the ghost all the chocolates and some champagne to make peace. The mirror begins in an upright position (see previous page). It then decides to put itself into other positions. Keep reading.

Art Illustration by Magdalena Adic and Kelly Schutz

HAUNTED MIRROR OR SOMETHING MOVING THE MIRROR?

PRINCE RUPERT SUITE

You can speculate that the MIRROR has loose screws and moves on its own due to walking vibrations and air movement in the room. However, it is also interesting to note that it would ONLY MOVE when my husband passed by it AND wasn't looking at it. Only in my view it would move. The truth be told, the MIRROR had been tightened nearly 10-12 times by me, the assistant manager, and cleaning staff prior to and during our stay.

The ghost loosens its screws on each side (see half way down) with ease and places itself into the position it wants to be in. See images following later in this chapter. You may ask, what caused the MIRROR to cycle round and round? Read my story near the end of this chapter. Slamming of the bathroom door and cycling of the mirror are just two events that occur in The Prince Rupert Suite. Keep reading, more is coming.

HAUNTINGS

What other areas of the hotel are haunted? Everywhere. Although the hauntings occur primarily in the 12th century section of the hotel, no area, including the cellar and newer areas are exempt from a ghostly encounter. There are several ghosts of various ages that roam this building.

1. **ROOM CHANGE**. Upon our arrival, we had a room change from the King James I Suite to the Prince Rupert Suite. We had wanted the Prince Philip Suite, but due its extreme haunted'ness, we were moved to the "next" most haunted.

2. **HALLWAY – STRONG MAGNETIC FIELD**. The reception staff walked with us to our room. As we went up the stairs, located near the reception desk, and made our way on the 2nd floor down a long hallway, one of the reception staff and I felt ourselves walking right into a very strong magnetic field. The field was so strong that it turned both of our faces bright red as a jolt of electricity passed through our bodies. We both commented about how "electrified" we felt from that moment as we reached the Prince Rupert Suite. It was a feeling like no other. Keep reading.

3. **PRINCE PHILIP SUITE – JILTED BRIDE (NO NAME).** A young lady dating back to the Victorian period has a tendency to "hang around" not only in the Prince Philip Suite but out in the hallway. She came to Shrewsbury to be married (date unknown). The day she was due to walk down the aisle, she discovered her husband to-be had run out on her and had married someone else. Mortified, she was so upset that she took her life by hanging herself

from the beams in the Prince Philip Suite, known as Room 5. See next page. She is seen on occasion in that room by unsuspecting guests.

Her hanging body has also appeared in the hallway. The Prince Philip Suite is located in the 12th Century section of the hotel. As reported to me by a hotel cleaning staff person during our stay, the hanging woman does not like the presence of a single man. For example, a painter was in the hallway a few years back working. He was minding his own business painting a wall when the hanging woman decided to appear behind him. Her feet were dangling behind his shoulder. As he caught a glimpse of her out of the corner of his eye, he became bewildered. It is not known if he finished his shift but he did tell a staff person, "I think this place is very sad and I will not be returning." In other words, HE QUIT.

The hung woman also likes to remove bedding and pillows from the bed hiding them in areas out of the room several feet away such as in the elevator lift (60 feet away).

The staff tries to book guests in this room that are not aware of the story behind this haunting.

She Hangs Here

Chairs, Table

Photo Taken by Kelly Renee Schutz
Prince Philip Suite, May 27, 2016

PRINCE PHILIP - TABLE AND CHAIRS. To the left, you will notice a table and chairs. It was reported by to me by the Assistant Manager and cleaning staff that on occasion, these chairs are turned around positioned to look OUT the window. This usually occurs after the cleaning staff has just left the room and is noticed by the Assistant Manager. It is as if "THEY" or "SOMEONE" is watching something outside.

93

PRINCE PHILIP - OBJECTS MOVED. Objects are moved in the room. At times, things are thrown in the room. A heavy feeling and cold breezes are felt.

DAVID BOYCE REPORT. As reported by and transcribed by David Boyce, a clairvoyant who lives in South Wales. On October 8, 2013, he stayed in the Prince Philip Suite a very short time and had an adrenaline rush. He arrived late to the hotel and needed a room. He did not know he would be staying in the most haunted room in the building. In fact, after this discovery and with all that he experienced, he requested a different room in the newer section of the hotel.

VISIONS. As Mr. Boyce was walking to his room, he saw and felt these visions: (a) a fighting and a male in an old uniform being speared in battle; (b) the sense of smoke from an old fire upstairs within the hotel which would have caused significant damage; (c) the feeling that people would have perished or died from smoke inhalation as a result of the fires fumes; (d) a young spirit of a girl wandering the corridors; (e) persons staying in the hotel would complain they smelled residual smoke in areas where none should be; (f) sense of a male who had fallen and tumbled down the stairs in the corridor and died from his injuries; (g) small young girl about

7 years old with long curly hair wearing what looked like an old homemade dress. Small white dog, looks like a Scottie, walking the corridor. Felt Anne might the be the child's name; (h) little girl may have been one of those who passed from smoke inhalation from a fire on the premises,

VISIONS IN PRINCE PHILIP SUITE. As David was in the Prince Philip Suite, he saw these visions: (a) he heard out loud, the name Mary Ellen, being called out by a male from the spirit world as if he were waiting for her to cross over to be with him again. Is this the name of the hanged woman? (b) while sitting on the bed upright with pillows behind him, he felt an intermittent breeze hit his right cheek. He could not determine where it came from and concluded it was not coming from the closed window or through the door that led into the conference area to his right-hand side. Stopped after several minutes; (c) felt constantly nauseas and dizzy with sick churning stomach, feeling as though someone was very nervous; (d) heart rate started racing and breathing became restricted as though someone was pushing on his upper chest; (e) spirit was showing him the gallows in the room near the right of the window as if dropping down to the street outside. Hanging feeling impressed upon him. There was something different to the left-hand side corner of the room as if it was a newer false ceiling.

(f) the name Mr. Hartnell was spoken from the spirit. (g) was shown a portly man who looks about 5'4" tall. He was wearing a waist coat and top hat. He was looking at his pocket watch attached to his waist coat on a chain. He seemed agitated as though he was waiting for someone who was late. He looked like an important person of the time. (h) smell of fresh flowers within the room when there were none anywhere.

Mr. Boyce didn't feel as though the spirits were dangerous or would hurt him. But when they are active, they are strong. A member of the staff had informed him an old original painting was hung on the wall within the present breakfast area prior to the hotel changing hands a few years back. It is believed the painting was sold and no longer within the hotel.

MORE HAUNTS

MY NAME IS MARTHA. According to the writings of Martin Wood, it was during the 1980's when a medium was staying at the hotel. The medium reported that she was going down the spiral staircase into the old kitchen when she had seen a young maid by the name of Martha. Martha had asked why gunshots were fired. The manager at the time knew they had no one working there by that name and stated there was no spiral staircase.

The manager said if gunshots were heard that the entire town would have been alerted. It was until present owner, Mike Matthews took over the hotel, that the discovery of a spiral staircase, constructed around the mid-1700's, that led to the old kitchen was discovered. Matthews had wanted to build a fitness center in that area. When they lifted the floorboards to lay foundation, they discovered a skeleton. The last known maid on record was named Martha. See her image on the next page.

SIDE NOTE: My ability to see ghosts is strengthening. I saw Martha in the hallway as we were walking to our room (Prince Rupert Suite). I caught a glimpse of her face, side view, skin tone as seen on next page, with short brown hair. I was not looking for or paying attention when this blurrrr caught my eye. She was rushing and vanished quickly. Yes, I really saw her.

According to the writings of Martin Wood, Martha was a quiet lady whose shadow was often seen standing in a corner in the kitchen [not clear if it is existing kitchen], just like a maid would have done. He says if you run your hand across the corner about 4 feet above the ground, he says, you can often feel a cold draft as if she is moving away.

Martha has also been seen in the ballroom as an energy orb. It has been mentioned when she manifests, she is holding a mop and bucket, as if she were to start cleaning.

Is This Martha, the Hotel Maid?

On the next page, to the right of the crooked stairways is The Prince Rupert Suite, where we stayed. The stairs leading upward go to the Prince Maurice's Suite. One of the cleaning staff told me she does not like going into that room because she feels sick, her energy is immediately drained, and she feels watched. These are symptoms of being attacked. If the entity in this room is angry, it will prey on a fearful person. My advice: (1) wear a cross, (2) say a protection prayer, (3) surround yourself with white light, (4) throw holy water on the floor upon entrance, and (5) ask that the entity not bother you. This may be the area where a fire occurred centuries ago. This room is in the 12th Century manor room section. This is also the area that Martha is seen walking the hallways. To the left, is a set of stairs that leads down to a fitness center. On the fitness center level is a door. Behind that door is a stone carved staircase that leads down into the cellar. Notice the mirror to the right of the stairs? Mirrors are major conductors to manifest hauntings.

PRINCE CHARLES SUITE. Next door to the Prince Philip Suite is the Prince Charles Suite. In a different period of time, a to-be groom took his life in that room when his to-be wife ran off with his best man. A co-worker, who was with David Boyce the evening of his experience, stayed in this room. He reported seeing an apparition appear to him. He didn't say anything to anyone for a long time for fear of being ridiculed.

THE FLANNEL NIGHTSHIRT GHOST. Some years ago, a film of *A Christmas Carol* was being made at Shrewsbury, with several of the film-crew staying at the Prince Rupert Hotel. A director, on his way to bed, saw an elderly man walking towards him wearing a flannel nightshirt. The director stood aside to allow him to pass. The phantom ghost nodded and vanished through a wall carrying a Wee Willy Winkie-type candle holder with a lit candle.

Photo Taken by Kelly Renee Schutz

BAR AREA ACROSS FROM RECEPTION. People have gone to the bar very late at night and upon entering the bar have noticed shadows and a black object hovering above.

ROOM 11. Guests have reported capturing many orbs in motion in this room.

PRINCE MAURICE ROOM. Guests have reported hearing footsteps above them (from Prince Rupert Suite) coming from this room when no one is there. The room is carpeted, which should muffle the sounds of footsteps – but – they are loud and clearly heard.

COLD SPOTS, FEELING WATCHED. Guests have reported seeing a black shadow figure standing next to a window by a conference room. Are they referring to the Prince Philip Suite? Have also reported when attempting to make contact with an apparition in one particular room, would hear Mary Elsbeth. Mary Elsbeth had a child out of wedlock and 2 other children. When asked questions, ghost equipment would respond by flickering. Notice the name is similar to that of David Boyce's report?

KING JAMES SUITE. When a sensitive guest went into this room, she felt that someone who hung about in there "didn't want her there." She did not notice until she walked around the bed the bedding on one side had been turned back. A sign to her, she went to a different room.

ASSISTANT MANAGER. Felt a feeling of something "brushing" on the back of her neck by something when alone working. Turned around and nothing was there.

FOOTSTEPS. Footsteps are heard walking behind staff and guests when no one is in the area or the environment appears peaceful. Some often heard on the 2nd floor.

RESTAURANT. The lights above us were flickering on and off when we ate dinner one evening. We were the only people in the restaurant. No other lights were flickering around us as we had a full view of more than half of the restaurant area and could see all lighting.

CELLAR BOY
Did This Young Boy Lead A Woman Back Safely?

LITTLE BOY, THOMAS. As written by Martin Wood, in the cellar of the Prince Rupert Hotel is the ghost of a small boy, most believe to be named Thomas. This young boy (see picture above) looks as if he dates to the Tudor period.

Many people have spotted Thomas standing by the outer retaining wall. On the other side of that wall, use to be a duck pond. It is alleged Thomas drowned in the Dock Pond. Not, "duck" ... "dock" pond. Water from the dock pond would run off down what is known as a dog pole and pass behind the houses on Wyle Cop before entering the river, Severn.

WOMAN LOST, HAND HELD. A woman, who became lost on one of the tours, reported that she felt it was Thomas who led her back to a familiar part of the hotel through its confusing hallways. In a mild panic, she felt as though his small hand took ahold of hers and as she tried to "clutch" a fist, was unable to because she felt the shape of a hand inside hers. She then felt herself being led by "someone" back to a familiar part of the building.

SCREAMING BOY. In another incident, not certain if Thomas, guests were awakened one night when they heard sounds of a young boy frantically trying to get into their room. The room reported was Room 1.

He was crying at the top of his lungs and the door knob was moving insinuating that he was trying to be let in or wanted in. When the guests came to the door and opened it, no one was there. His screams were frightening.

STONE CELLAR – TURNED INTO WINE CELLAR

THE CHOKING GHOST. As viewed in the YouTube video, Martin Wood, local historian, was giving a small tour of the cellars when he began talking about the unfriendly, angry man (ghost) who didn't like him or too many people standing in "his" room. On occasion, tourists have heard him telling them "to leave." (they do). This angry man likes to put the feeling of his hands around people's necks (choking). A woman, who was standing at the top of a stairs, squealed as she caught her necklace of green stones before it fell to the floor. The woman said she felt as though someone were unscrewing it. No one was behind her. She left the tour.

KNOCKS ON DOORS. Some guests have reported hearing knocks on their doors only to find no one there. Guests have left their lights and televisions on all evening to drown out any noises they proclaim to hear in their rooms or outside their doors. In my attempt to turn our television on, around 3:30 AM, with our lights on by the way, our remote was dead. Apparitions like to drain the batteries of remote controls. All I can say is, I wish they left ours alone.

WALLPAPER IN ROOM 1. When the wallpaper was being removed in Room1, it was noticed that there would be a lot of ghostly activity. Ghosts do not like change.

HAUNTINGS IN PRINCE RUPERT SUITE

Photo of Prince Rupert
Artwork Displayed in Lobby Near Lift

For those who have stayed in the Prince Rupert Suite and had an experience, I applaud you. My husband and I will never forget our time in this room. This room demonstrated that an 82% moon phase can bring about extreme activity. Or, in this case, it may not matter at all. We stayed in this room on May 27, 2016.

INCIDENTS IN PRINCE RUPERT SUITE

1. As of our visit, this room has 4 mirrors that surround every angle. Ghostly activity thrives with mirrors in a room.

2. Most frequent, the SLAMMING of the bathroom door. Although the entrance leading into the bathroom is sloped downward, this slope is not enough force to slam a door. Ghosts love to slam doors. We placed a luggage rack against it to avoid slamming or shutting.

3. IMAGE in wardrobe mirror no one can figure out.

THEORY OF ODD SHAPED LINE. My husband seems to think that this odd marking that follows the oval pattern of the mirror is a reflection of its edges. What you cannot see is that at the bottom, it twists into a hanging noose. Others have captured this image. I have captured it with and without a flash. It projects onto the door that leads into the room. I would be curious to know what the glass is made out of and if there is anything behind that glass to cause this image reflecting outward.

4. Imprints of BUTT on the bed or HANDS on the pillow are common. You can't see them, but the hand prints are on my pillow (left hand side). Husband looks unaffected, huh. Take a look at the REAL ORB that is on the mirror of the wardrobe (to the left). The entity in this room likes to sit on the bed toward the end. Never noticed hand prints.

5. Ghost in this room likes to move the pillows.

6. Ghost in this room does not like the maintenance people coming in, period. When our lamp wasn't working, one had to attempt to go into that room. However, before the ghost lets anyone in, you have to ask permission when entering. My lamp (left side) was not working and it was not clear if it were a bulb issue. I had intended to leave it on all night. When husband and I were at dinner, our key was requested by the assistant manager because the ghost would not let the maintenance person into our room. In fact, the ghost pushes back on the door. Common occurrence. You may be thinking - oh, the maintenance person put his hand prints all over my pillow when he was tampering with the lamp. Nope. You didn't see how the hand prints were displayed on the pillow – like a crime scene.

7. Within 15 minutes of our being in the room, I began having a headache and not feeling 100%. The air felt heavy and it didn't feel right. After walking through the electromagnetic field in the hallway, it was as though my ability to feel or sense spirits was coming to life. I will sequence some pictures for you so you can understand what we (I) went through. When ghosts how themselves, they do not often show to more than one person. Because I am

extremely open, something can happen right in front of you and the other person won't see. Here is a mini-journey of pictures.

ENTERING THE ROOM – NOTICE THE MIRROR STRAIGHT UP. NO HAND PRINTS PILLOWS. NO BUTT PRINT ON BED. AFTER SUPPER, DIFFERENT STORY.

HUSBAND BLESSES THE ROOM WITH HOLY WATER

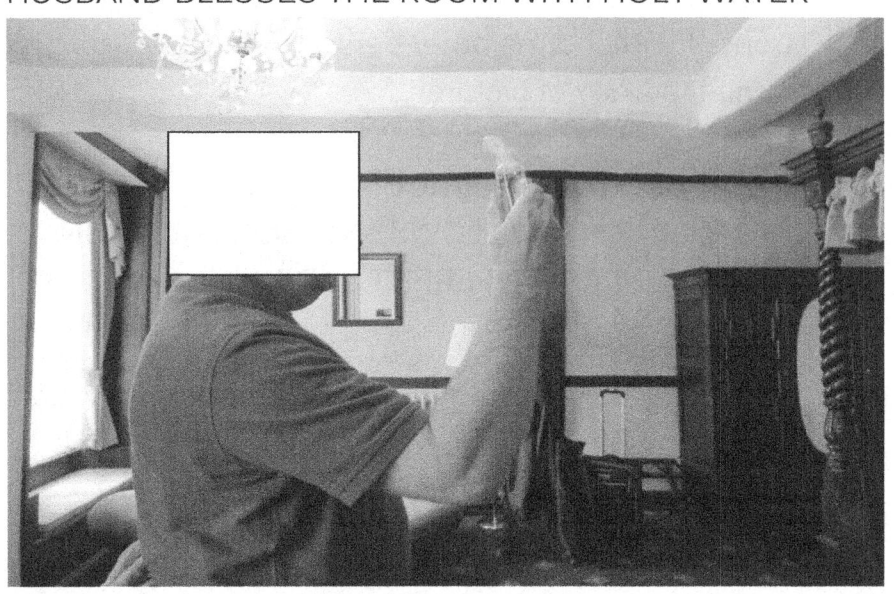

LOOKS CALM AND UNEVENTFUL DOESN'T IT?

NO ACTIVITY, SO IT SEEMS

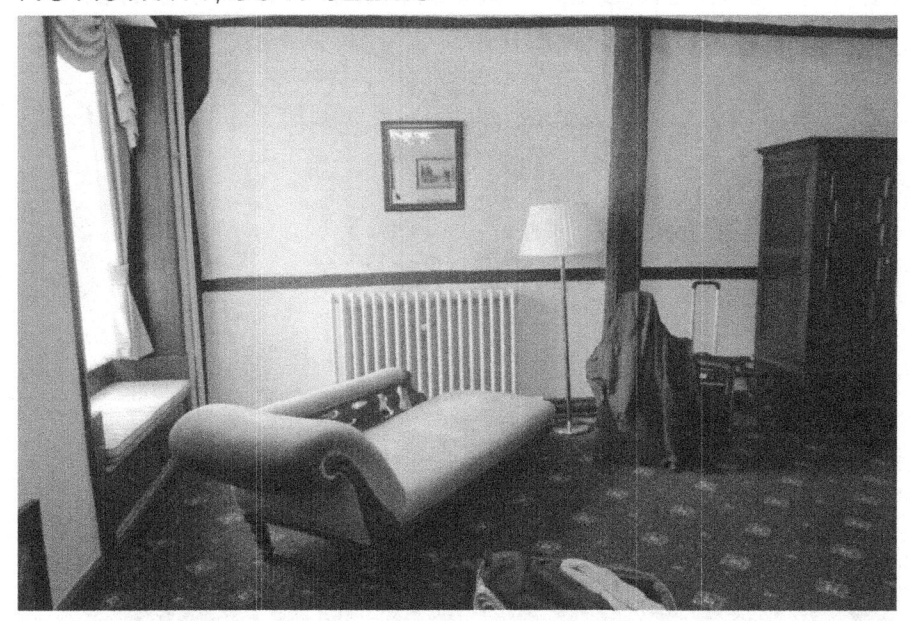

ACITIVITY BEFORE DINNER – TWO ORBS ON BED

BEFORE DINNER, ORB ON SOFA WAITING PATIENTLY

BEFORE DINNER, ORB NEAR CEILING - SOLID

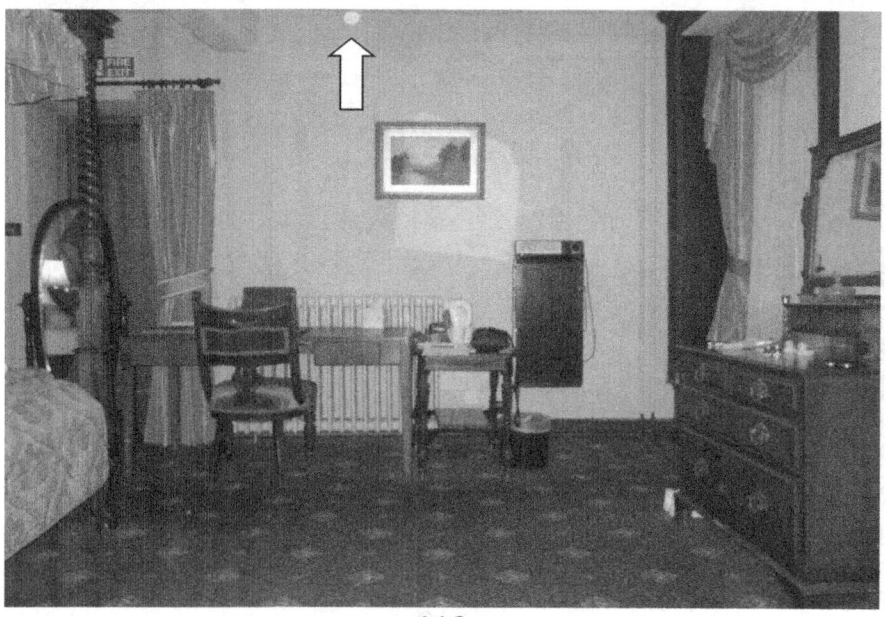

AFTER DINNER, WE FIND THE MIRROR LIKE THIS

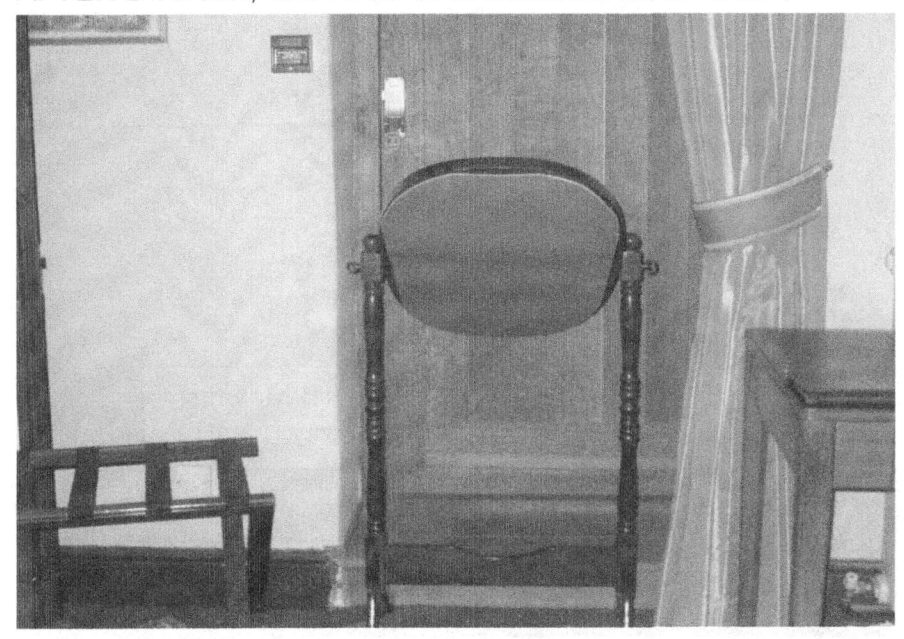

BEFORE BED, ORB IS SOLID. HUSBAND UNAFFECTED.

My K2 Meter
Never Blinked

BEFORE BED, ORB MOVING AWAY. HUSBAND
UNAFFECTED.

ORB Moving
Away (Faint)

SIDE NOTE: When we arrived back from dinner, I have to
admit, I was skeptical of the maintenance man. I thought
he might have put the hand prints on the pillow and
moved the mirror.

MIRROR WAS TIGHTENED. However, this did not
happen. The mirror had been tightened several times.
Tightened to the point where it could not move easily or at
all. However, the ghost didn't like the STRAIGHT UP mirror
and kept moving it. When my husband would walk past it,
it would move [because he would not see it and I would;
no, it wasn't a vibration causing it to move, it almost
appeared like a joke to the ghost to do this when he
wasn't paying attention]. See image next page.

READY FOR BED – TERROR. At 1:30 PM-2:00 AM, my husband wanted to go to bed. He took the holy water from his dresser and he started to say the IN NAME OF CHRIST protection prayer. I was standing on my side of the bed looking at the mirror. He was standing at the foot of the bed with his body TURNED AWAY from the mirror. As soon as he started saying that prayer, the mirror JOLTED, like a race horse coming out of its gate at a race and began **CYCLING ROUND (Full Circle).** I stood there terrified and looked white (says my husband). When I said, "LOOK" ... it had stopped in the position I am showing you in the next picture.

CYCLING MIRROR. I have video of this mirror moving. From the moment we arrived, I couldn't take my eyes off of the oval mirror. I felt there was something odd about it. Let me remind you that the mirror has been repositioned in this room. In 2012, it was in front of a wall and window on the other side of the room. During our stay, it was positioned in front of an exit door with lots of space behind it to CYCLE. I questioned if ghosts were coming and going through the exit door moving the mirror. I questioned if that oval mirror, which directly faces the wardrobe, had double the power to manifest ghostly entities. I had questioned if someone had taken a strong possession over that room finding comfort in sitting and sleeping on the bed. Mirrors absorb energy. What is its story?

THIS IS HOW THE MIRROR LIKES ITS POSITION

TERRIFED COULDN'T SLEEP. I put a black mask over my face because the incident threw me into a very severe panic attack. I was burning up, red in the face, labored breathing. I hate to even admit this, but the ghost was hovering over my face for several minutes and its "freezing" temperature helped me to settle down a little and feel better. I just asked it wouldn't hurt me. My husband was snoring the entire time. Typical of ghost experiences. Reports have also stated that people would feel a cool breeze over their face or something blowing gently into their ear. I fell asleep around 4:00 AM ... I gave up and passed out.

THE WARDROBE. The wardrobe in that room, that has the strange image in its glass, is a very old piece. In 2012, during the news reporting tour of that room, it was behind the sofa. When we were there, it was facing the oval mirror. The wardrobe is not loose enough to open by itself. You will see in looking at it (next page), that it was open about 1" when I woke up the next day.

With 4 hours of sleep, for some reason, it is possible the ghost sleeps or resides in the wardrobe. When the orb was in the mirror and leaving it (see previous images), the door was closed.

CANDLESTICK. The gold candlestick was moved to an odd position on the dresser with mirror.

TRIGGER OBJECTS. None of my trigger objects were touched or moved.

MANAGEMENT AND CLEANING STAFF. Were brought in the next day and shown what the mirror had done in front of me [us]. I was in error in my report about which side of the mirror was actually "up" – cork down, mirror up. The cleaning staff told both of us that she had been having incidents with the mirror in the past few days. Every time she would straighten it or was bent over, it would hit her. Hit her where? Where do you think? Do you think offering a chocolate matters to the apparition(s) in the room?

Chapter 8
Spiritual, Para-, Extra-, or Ultra-terrestrial?

Art Illustration by Kelly Renee Schutz

Chapter 8
Spiritual, Para-, Extra-, or Ultra-terrestrial?

BACKGROUND

As of present, there seems to be chatter in the paranormal community on whether experiences we have are caused by: (1) our own being (tulpas), (2) spiritual, (3) extraterrestrial, or (4) ultra-terrestrial. I am most certain that by the time I publish this book ... there will be yet another phenomena level to ponder.

Very few citizen researchers are confident enough to know the difference between these phenomena. I have been on my own mission for years to figure out which phenomena I have experienced. Just about the time I think I know ... something happens that confuses my thinking.

The consensus overall (for now) is that it appears there may be an overlap between these phenomena categories. The question remains ... how can you tell where the overlap begins and ends?

DEFINITIONS

Extraterrestrial – of or from outside the earth or its atmosphere. For example, aliens from an off-earth planet.

They (aliens) hide from us in various ways and are often disguised (or try to be) as *Black-Eyed Children or Men in Black*. **Terrestrial** – is of, relating to, or inhabiting the land of the earth or its inhabitants. For example, a creature that has always been on this earth but may not always show in true physical form. An example might be a trickster [taking the form of an animal or something else]. Does not live in the water, trees, or in the air. Shows up out of thin air (parallel universe) and disappears. **Ultra-Terrestrial** – are an alien race that isn't really alien. The race originated from Earth, just like humans, but their civilization is much older and advanced than ours. They have no issue hiding from us but are not easily captured. Some say this alien race can hide in the hollow parts of the Earth or even on the back side of the moon. They co-exist with humans. They can be visible and have abilities to be invisible. For example, *Moth Man and Big Foot*. **Spiritual** – simply stated, a divine spirit. Most believe spiritual visitations are from loved ones. **Tulpas** – are entities generated from a person's mind. For example, a bit different from an imaginary friend, a tulpa has intelligence, can think on its own, can express emotions, and has memories.

MY PERSONAL EXAMPLES

There is no doubt I have been evolving in my abilities and encounters/visitations. However, for years, I may have been mislabeling my experiences. Let me give you three (of many) examples as to why I feel one should not jump to immediate conclusions about their experiences.

EXAMPLE 1 – the handprint [see Chapter 11]. I am a religious and spiritual person. I believe in God but I also believe there are other forces among us on and away from our planet. I do believe my guardian angels guide me daily but I also believe I have attachments from "something" that give me occasional judgment and direction advice [not sure about protection].

The night before this blood red handprint showed on my body, I smelled a strong, rose-water perfume (thought it was my husband's shampoo). I felt incredibly nauseated. The smell was so strong, I pulled the covers over my nose. The next morning, this long-fingered handprint (upside down) with a crooked finger was burned (bruised deeply) into my chest. It took 3 hours for it to disappear. Some would ask me if my grandmother visited. I would respond, "no, this wasn't the perfume she wore." My immediate thought started with **spiritual** but then went to **extraterrestria**l (the way the fingers looked). It could have been someone else's hand **(spiritual or paranormal)**. Maybe it was **ultra-terrestrial**? I did dream about (another time) a mantis being. Today, my conclusion is inconclusive though I lean in the direction of **extraterrestrial**.

EXAMPLE 2 – Las Vegas hotel visit. Just before I lied down in my hotel room, I looked out the window (60th floor) and said, "gee, I wonder if I will be able to see any alien UFO crafts from this high up?"

When I lied down to go to bed, my lights started to flicker. At first, I thought the light system was malfunctioning (panel operated). Then, there came two knocks behind my head (on the wall). The room behind my bedroom was my bathroom. I was the only person in the room.

Deep down inside my thought went to having a **paranormal** experience. I never believed in UFO's or aliens. The next day when I woke up, I felt very unusual (like my blood had been refreshed). I thought this feeling was odd. An incident similar to this one happened one other time in my bedroom at home. Never since.

A couple years later, after having poltergeist activity in my home, I had a UFO experiencer-psychic over to my house to check it out and to give me a reading. Not knowing anything about my Las Vegas stay, she brought up in her reading a situation I was in where I had an alien visitation. She told me the visitation occurred in a hotel room one evening where an alien/extraterrestrial force was checking my blood. It was there to check me out, not to cause harm to me. It just so happens a couple months after that incident in the Las Vegas room, I was diagnosed with cancer. The doctor told me I was a miracle (with emphasis). Looking back, I initially believed my experience was **paranormal**. Now I feel strongly that what I experienced that night was **extraterrestrial**. I may never know.

EXAMPLE 3 – faces in the window screen [Chapter 4]. When I photographed the two apparitions in the screened window in 2007, I believed these entities were my great aunt and great grandfather. After all, my great grandfather built the house. It only seemed logical that he would show in the window. My great aunt passed away two miles down the road. She showed around age 6 (passed at age 10). It would only be logical they would be traveling together. However, a psychic told me once that the man above her in that window may have been her doctor [apparently devastated by her death]. In fact, I found a picture of the doctor who seemed to match the image in the window. Will always be inconclusive.

I heard telepathically (two days later when I went back to the house) to check the genealogy. It is true, I mislabeled her image in the family history. I was able to match her facial and hair features to a picture I had of her. I believed what I experienced was **spiritual or paranormal.**

This example demonstrates one aspect about our beliefs and experiences. We want to believe our relatives come back to visit us. However, how am I so sure that what I experienced visually (via photograph) was a demonic trickster wanting to break down my vulnerabilities to get me back onto that property? Did I have experiences since? Yes. Was I ever attacked on that property? Yes. Do I believe these apparition images were tricksters? No.

I ruled out **extraterrestrial and ultra-terrestrial** situations because it just didn't feel like anything of this nature. However, unless they come out of the house to introduce themselves to me ... even then, you can't always believe what you see. This example lends itself to the MANY situations where tricksters act like children or sound like babies crying [or other human sounds] to get people to walk into their traps. As humans, this only goes to show that we gravitate toward our beliefs first and then, we start to question them. We want to believe spirits will not harm us. We want to believe God is always with us. We want to believe there is nothing of a higher power that will toy with us. Take a look at the image below – which category would you put it in?

Illustration Mixed Media by Kelly Renee Schutz

Chapter 9
Waking Up with Clothes Backwards

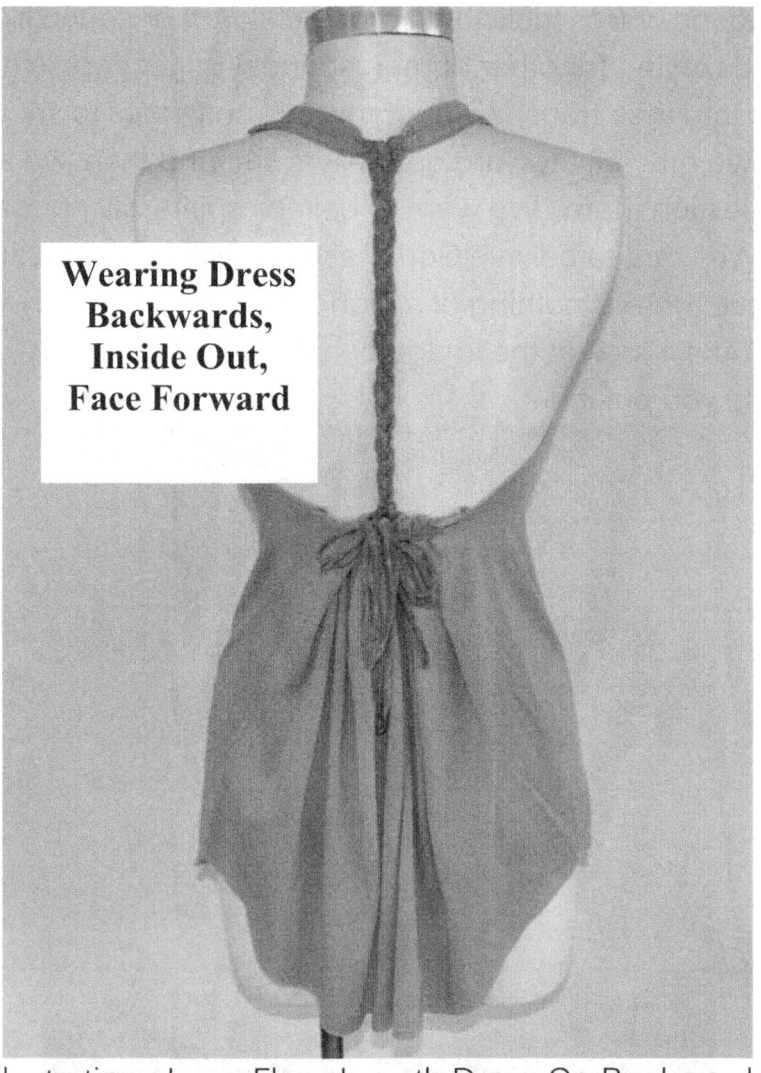

Wearing Dress Backwards, Inside Out, Face Forward

Illustration - Long Floor-Length Dress On Backwards

Chapter 9
Waking Up with Clothes Backwards

BELIEF

Some believe if you wake up from your sleep with your pajamas or other clothes on backwards that you may have been abducted and returned by an alien species. Aliens do not necessarily share our mannerism in how we wear our clothes nor do they care about redressing. In some cases, one might find their clothes removed from their body and/or pillowcases removed from their pillows to be puddled between, next to, or at the end of the bed.

MY EXPERIENCES

I can count on one hand the times I have awakened from my sleep to find my clothes on backwards, inside out, and/or removed. I would find my clothes lying near my feet and/or on a chair next to me. There have also been two occasions when my husband's pillowcase would be removed from his head during the night while he was sleeping and puddled between us. Discovering this and puzzled, we would always ask the question, "what happened last night?"

SLEEPWALKING

Could these experiences be of another nature -- extraterrestrial or sleepwalking? According to an article found on the Internet, sleepwalking, also called somnambulism, occurs when a sleeper leaves the bed and performs complex behaviors without fully waking up.

Typical sleepwalking behaviors include walking, talking, running, rummaging through drawers, picking up objects, getting ready for school, preparing breakfast, eating, or putting on/changing clothes.

The person who is sleepwalking may have their eyes open but have significantly reduced awareness of their surroundings and limited ability to interact with those around them.

The article continues to say a sleepwalking episode usually occurs early in the night and lasts just a few minutes, though sleepwalking can last up to 40 minutes or even hours.

BREAKING DOWN MY EXPERIENCES

In review of the following situations, tell me which ones you think are extraterrestrial and/or sleepwalking episodes.

INCIDENT #1 – I am 24 years old. I experience high anxiety. To calm my nerves, I like snacking on mini-Snickers bites and tapioca snack packs (back then, eaten from a tin can with pull off lid). One morning, I awaken to discover 20 mini-Snicker wrappers on my chest.

On another night (mid-morning hours), I awaken to find myself licking the lid of a tapioca snack pack can (sharp edges). Obviously, these two examples are related to a sleep disorder.

INCIDENT #2 – I am 28 years old. I live in a house with 3 other girls. I live on the main floor just outside of the kitchen. Sounds from the kitchen travel easily through the walls into my room. Because my room was extremely cold in winter, I decided to get a heated waterbed. Being heated, I didn't feel the need to wear pajamas. One evening, while sleeping, I must have heard a noise and subconsciously felt the need to put some clothes on. When I woke up in the morning, I found myself wearing a long formal dress (from my closet), backwards and inside out. How I was able to get into it with the zipper up is beyond me.

Was this situation extraterrestrial or sleepwalking? In that house, I believed the basement was haunted (never went down there). I never believed the rest of the house had haunting issues. I didn't believe in extraterrestrials back then. I believe this was a sleepwalking incident caused by my feeling conscious about not wearing anything while sleeping. If I would have been discovered not wearing any clothes, I would have felt embarrassed. Over the years, I would have frequent dreams about my not wearing any clothes around people and trying to hide behind something to not be viewed.

INCIDENT #3 – We are in our mid-40's. My husband and I are sleeping. In the morning, we awaken to find his pillowcase from the pillow he lies on removed completely and puddled between us. This is confusing as this has never happened before. We did live in a haunted house during this time. The night before (mid-morning), around 2:00 AM, we did awaken from our sleep to see our television on (no picture) and making-showing that static sound. This scared both of us as the television was turned off when we went to sleep. This situation – the puddled pillowcase and the static television, we believe, were paranormal.

INCIDENT #4 – We are in our early 50's. One morning, different home, I am awakened to find my pajamas lying on a chair down by the foot of my bed. On another night, I found them lying in a chair next to my bed. On another night, my husband and I discovered, once again, his pillowcase puddled between us. I need to take note here … he doesn't move much when he sleeps. This is highly unusual. Could any of these have been extraterrestrial in nature?

INCIDENT #5 – I discover a blood red handprint on my body after I awaken (bedroom). Read Chapter 11.

INCIDENT #6 – I hear what sounds like a snow shovel scraping against a sidewalk in the middle of our bedroom at 3:00'sh AM. No one is shoveling.

We hear the same sound while eating (in our livingroom) at 7:00 PM. (different night). No one in sight. Nothing internal. Nothing external. So, what is making this sound?

INCIDENT #7 – I am now 60 years old. I have a dream about who I thought was my husband's niece. On a radio program, I said cousin. I need to correct this and say, "niece." In my vivid dream, his niece was standing with her back towards me. When she turned around, she appeared to me as a mantis being (humanoid) wearing a black COVID mask. Scared out of my mind, I woke up in a massive sweat with my heart racing.

Were Any of These Situations Spiritual, Paranormal, Extraterrestrial, or due to a Sleep Disorder?
Not all were due to a sleep disorder.

QUESTION
When was the last time I had an unusual episode similar to the ones described above?

ANSWER
The last episode, as of this writing, that was unusual was the mantis being dream. I feel my experiences are evolving and cannot be explained.

Tales of Apparitions #2

Chapter 10
Twinberry Lane

Art Illustration by Kelly Renee Schutz
Tales of Apparitions

Chapter 10
Twinberry Lane

"Wow, what is that?" he said. "I don't think you want to go inside of that building," I replied. "Why not?" he comments. "Most people regret it and don't have a very good time in it," I expressed.

"That building doesn't frighten me, look at it," he proclaimed. "That's from the outside ... the inside is much different," I said. "What could be so bad inside?" I said.

"Fine, well then, pick a door and go inside. I need to forewarn you though, you will be able to enter through either door but will have a difficult time trying to find your way out," I expressed. "I use to be a boy scout, doesn't look that complicated. I got this," he boasted.

The man with a brave spirit enters the building but is not seen for four days. When he finally comes out, he is dirty, unable to describe his experience, and is emotionless. What was most apparent was his lack of confidence. Going in, he appeared to be a regular tough guy. Coming out, he acted like a shaken school girl.

Unlike most people who feel invincible going into a building of uncertainty, most proclaim when they finally come out, they will never step foot inside again.

The structure on Twinberry Lane is like no other. It was built by a man who wanted to take amusement to a higher level of consciousness. The man passed away years ago but asked that I watch over the structure not allowing the city to tear it down. It remains in the same spot he built it on. Sort of sits there like a lone duck. Sometimes, an eye sore. Life has since built itself around it.

I feel it is my duty to honor his wishes to let people go inside of it. However, as much as I forewarn people about it, many think it is nothing more than a building that takes up space on a street. Being mysterious intrigues people but doesn't seem to evoke fear. My being the keeper of its mystery, I made an oath to fulfill this man's mission to shake people up while allowing their consciousness to rise to a new level.

The structure was built during the 1920's when side shows at fairs were popular drawing crowds of people. People were intrigued by mystery and oddities. This gave this man an idea to create something that would amuse people with trickery. It was his intention to build something that would confuse the mind and mislead the soul. Most go inside expecting the opportunity to prove something to themselves. To bring out their fears. To conquer confusion. Many thrill seekers like being scared and rarely believe they would succumb to their weakest part of themselves, their soul.

From the outside, the building looks like it has two doors, four windows, and two levels. Once inside, it's like being in a maze at a carnival. To reveal the mystery of what is inside would be giving away its dark secrets.

Most people do not want to know how a magic trick works because they want to be thrilled by the experience. This experience is no different. It provides the same or greater experience than being at an amusement park.

Relating this to the paranormal, same idea. Once you discover what you are thrilled to seek, it doesn't have the same feeling once the hunt is over.

"That's it? Nothing more to say about this building?" the intrigued man says. "Yes, that's all I can say."

"Therefore, what will it be? Do you still want to go inside or do you wish to just stand here and look at it?"

To discover the answer? Response: "I'll think we should both just stand here and look at it. Let the mystery of it continue."

Chapter 11
Blood Red HandPrint

Illustration by Halida Dwi Edyati

Chapter 11
Blood Red HandPrint

PHENOMENA

You lie down in bed to fall asleep for the evening. You smell a light flowery perfume scent drift over your face. You are lying on your side facing your husband. As you continue to smell the flowery scent, it becomes repulsive. You speculate the smell is from a cheap shampoo used by your husband. You turn over on your other side and pull the covers over your nose to reduce the smell.

The next morning, you drag yourself out of bed and walk into the bathroom. You look at yourself in the mirror and notice a blood red handprint above your chest area. The handprint is upside down. For the first few minutes, you are in disbelief as to what you are seeing. As you study the handprint, you notice a hook on one of the fingers (see pages 139-140). As you press down on the handprint, the indentation from your pressure shows "white" not "red". You rule out the likelihood your hand caused the print creating the blood red color.

Where did this handprint come from? It took three hours for the handprint to disappear from your body. A few months later, the same handprint shows up on your dusty topped nightstand. Is someone trying to give you a message? Good message or a warning?

WORD OF WARNING – GRAPHIC PICTURES

IMAGE 1 – Upside Handprint with Hooked Finger

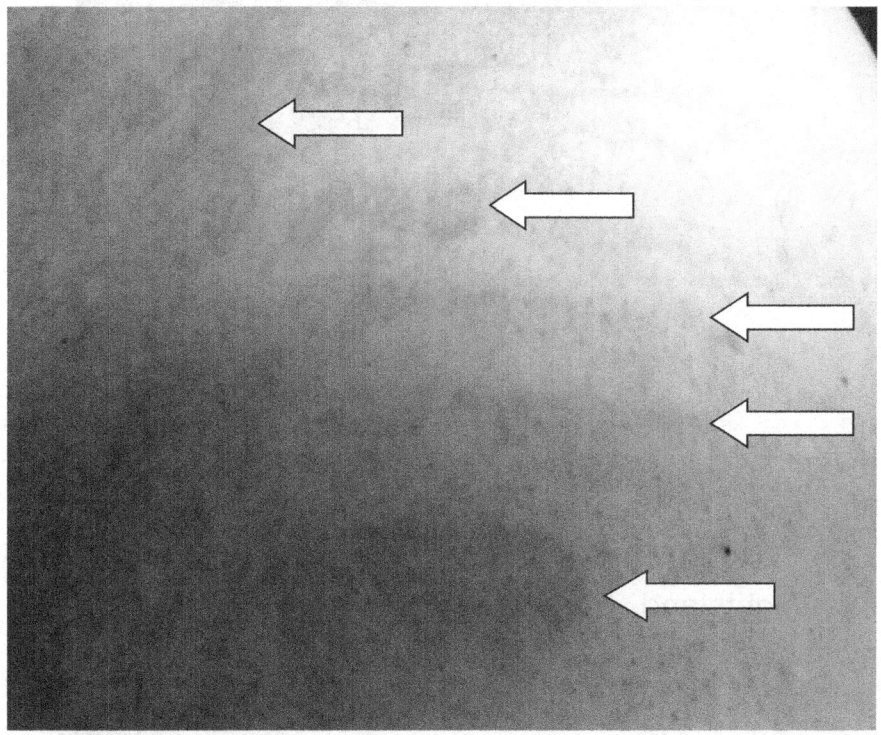

Difficult to see image because was photographed near a bright window. Handprint above chest area (blood red). Discovered on body June 27, 2020. Disappeared over three hours. Upside down. Long-fingered. Stretched.

The second finger down from the left shows an unusual hook in its top digit (compare to dresser image page 140).

Image taken morning after I smelled light sweet repulsive perfume scent as I was falling asleep near my husband. He was ruled out.   139

IMAGE 2 – Handprint on Body and Scratches on Neck

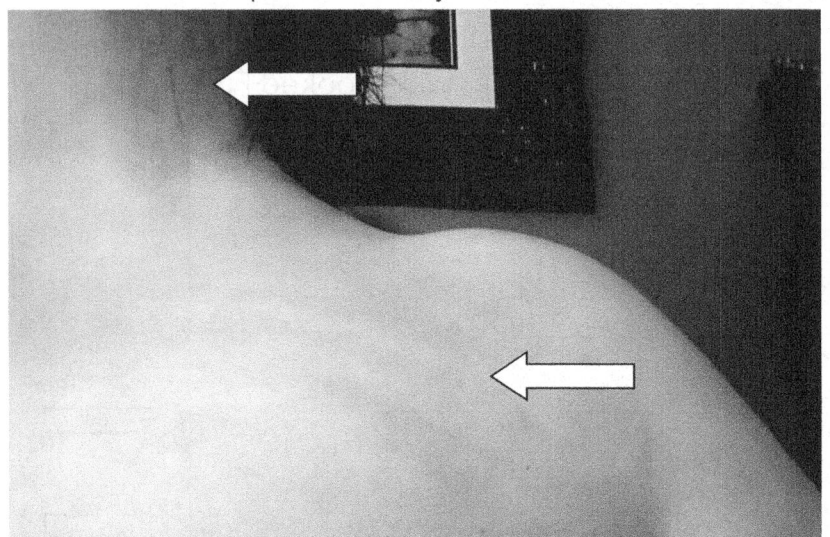

Image difficult to see as taken against bright light. Two-three scratches near neck (see top arrow). Handprint (long marking) above chest. Picture below, handprint on dusty nightstand. Compare. Hooked finger is odd. <u>Not</u> my hand. Scratches on neck inconclusive.

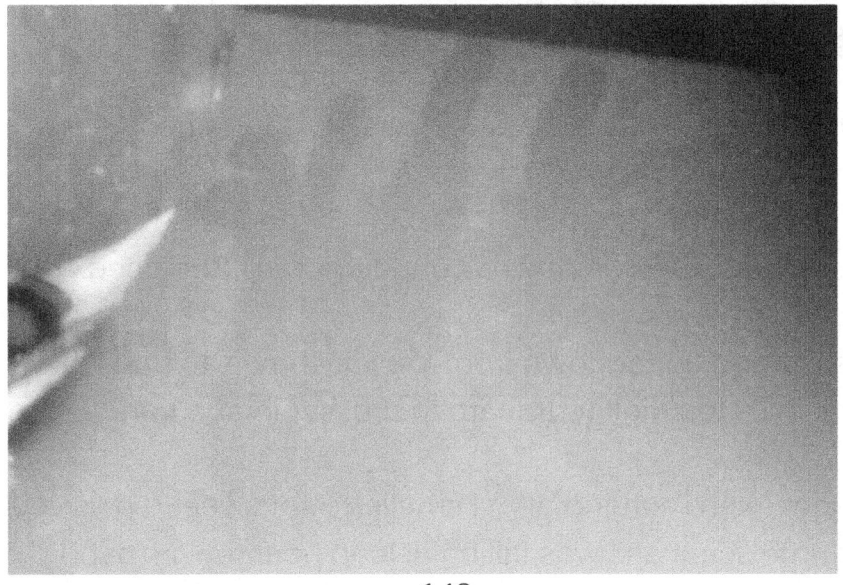

DEFINITIONS

Apparition – an unusual or unexpected sight or situation; materialization just after manifestation. **Alien Contactee** – people who have experienced contact (physical or otherwise) with extraterrestrials or disembodied spirits. **Handprint** – clients of therapists who indicated they have these markings appear on their bodies most often feel unhappy, lost, or deprived of hope for the future. Spirit attachment could happen to anyone, including young children and babies. **High Sensitivity** – physical, acute, mental, and emotional responses to internal or external stimuli. **Spirit Attachment** – common symptoms of spirit attachment can be both mental and physical.

CASES OF MARKINGS UNCLEAR

When a person is marked by something unexplainable, it can be rather confusing. In most cases, people want to find answers. Especially if the mark occurred while the person was sleeping. What does a handprint mark mean? Who marked me? Why was I marked? Is this mark a sign of communication from a loved one or spirit guide? Worse yet, from a negative or hostile force?

RESEARCH

I attempted to research handprint markings. I did not have much luck or was looking in the wrong places for answers. I have read numerous blogs from people who discovered handprints on their own, children, teens, and baby's bodies. Findings from source inconclusive.

141

OUR OWN HANDS. Handprint markings discovered on objects, walls, mirrors, cars, etc. are "usually" explainable. In many of these situations, prints (marks) that were once "invisible" to the naked eye can surface on objects during different points in time due to environmental changes. The culprit responsible for initially placing these marks (our hands) emits oils into the surface-objects.

However, when a blood red handprint mark shows up on a body (adults, teens, children, babies) and remains on the body for a period of time ... we sit up and take notice. When marks show up on backs, fronts, chests, legs, and sometimes, even faces, we become alarmed. In these cases, we rule out the "oils from our hands" theory.

HOOKED FINGER. The handprint that showed palm up (upside down) on my chest showed stretched fingers with one digit having a hooked finger. Reports from others regarding the duration of their markings lasted anywhere from 1 hour to 2 weeks. My marking remained blood red for about 2 hours until it finally began fading and disappearing around 3 hours.

My research found less than 1000 people reporting their stories in a blog on the Internet. Similar situation to mine. Unsuspecting place on their or family member's body. I would suspect more cases have occurred but have not been reported (I never reported mine). The question, of course, is "who or what created this mark?"

QUEST TO FIND ANSWERS

In my own quest searching for answers, I would be unable to find one. I could not even speculate at this point. I reached out to a few credible psychics. Answer ... "have no idea." It seemed like no one was willing to throw their idea into the ring on this one.

Of course, my questions remain ... "Whose marking is it?" "Why was it on me?" "Is there something I need to know?" "Did it come from a loved one or from someone hateful? Will I ever find out? Probably not.

QUESTIONS/THOUGHTS

Some people look at their handprint mark as a sign from a loved one, God, or guardian angel. Some feel the handprint marking gives them a sense of comfort while others, like myself, are highly suspicious. Are handprint markings a sign of warning or communication attempt?

HANDPRINT ON DUSTY NIGHTSTAND

I am fully aware I will not be winning an award for "housecleaner of the year." In review of the handprint marking on the nightstand (page 39), it appeared similar to the one that showed on my chest. Was I SURE it was not from my own hand? I do not think so. Read on.

And "yes" ... I clean the nightstand more frequently now.

NIGHTSTAND. The handprint mark discovered on my dusty nightstand was noticed a few months after the handprint on my body. It went unnoticed because (1) I am a terrible dust cleaner, and (2) I unknowingly place my water bottles over the area where the handprint showed. In other words, a habit that goes unnoticed. Until enough dust collected. It just so happens, one night, I lifted one of my water bottles and saw the marking. In lifting the other bottle, I noticed the full handprint WITH hooked finger.

ATTACHMENT. It just so happens I was listening to a paranormal radio show where a couple (experts) were talking about how they can remove attachments. They were also discussing how attachments can affect people. I thought to myself, "here is my opportunity to get my questions answered." I contacted the experts and scheduled them for an interview to be on my radio show.

WHOSE HAND IS ON MY BODY?

PSYCHIC. Before I scheduled the interview with the attachment experts, I decided to reach out to one more psychic to ask, "do you know how a handprint mark ended up on my chest?"

The psychic told me she felt it was of a woman who felt lost. A woman who followed me home, attached itself, and finds comfort being on me. [seriously, get off].

EXPERTS. When I brought the psychic's claim to the attention of the experts (lost woman), they had told me that I did not have ONE ... but rather ... SIXTEEN attachments on my body. They also mentioned, as a subtle comparison, that Hollywood personalities (not me) and musicians seem to have a lot more (50+) on their bodies. Would this explain their hidden skills and talents?

REACTION. My reaction was, "are you sure?" I did not get around to asking where they all came from or who they were. Just hearing you have SIXTEEN hitchhikers on your body makes you wonder. After all, I am very much aware I am a pied piper of attracting apparitions, children, and dogs. But ... I have never felt these "attachments" on me ... so how could I confirm they were? How would I know?

SELFISH. As a side note, I had been winning lots of jackpots at casinos in the past few years and did not want the experts to remove the "gambler" attachment from me. I know ... I know. Ridiculous. What if these attachments had nothing to do with my winning jackpots?

16 ATTACHMENTS REMOVED

How does one know if something is attached to them? In my having SIXTEEN attachments on me (so I was told) ... I never felt anything. Some people encounter personality changes [anger, depression, loneliness, suicidal thoughts]. Others discover talents-skills that do not run in their family genetics. Others may blame their failing health on family genetics or poor eating. 145

I have heard one should "sage" themselves on occasion to remove attachments. However, in my case, I was a bit uncertain as to "if" I had any to begin with and I was certainly not wanting any "lucky ones" to be removed.

ATTACHMENT EXPERTS

I am rather skeptical when it comes to people claiming they have a "specialized" expertise. After all, who has ever heard of an attachment expert? Not my first rodeo.

The closest I would be able to come in making a similarity would be that of a Reiki therapist. Someone who works with energy and can draw negative energy out of a person's body. This I can verify as a method that works.

An attachment expert may have psychic abilities. They may also have Reiki abilities. But ... how is this going to work in removing my attachments from ME when the experts live 1500-2000 miles away?

Okay, I will bite. This was just another notch in my belt trying to solve a paranormal mystery. That and I wanted answers ... "who or what was this handprint?"

QUESTION/THOUGHTS

I was very skeptical with this "magical" process of removing attachments from afar. After all, if you cannot feel them to begin with ... how will you know if they are off you? That question (by me) would soon be answered.

RADIO SHOW. I host and produce a top ranked paranormal radio show. I was preparing to interview the attachment removal experts. The night before their interview, as I was sleeping, the removal arrived.

THE REMOVAL. I sleep like the dead. At some point during the middle of the night, I found myself sitting half-way up in bed in a trance-like state. This was odd because I usually cannot do a sit up let alone hold one for more than a half a second.

I was not fully awake at any point. As I was angled up, I vaguely recall my mouth opening with bunches of air being vomited out. I remained in a trance-like state and sleep. This was NOT a typical experience for me. In fact, it was something I have never experienced before.

I do recall one of the experts saying "his sister, the gifted attachment expert" would be "working on me" at some point. This point in time was not revealed.

I recalled the attachment expert saying to me when attachments "come out" or "come off" of a person ... they often resist.

FLASHBACK. This reminded me of the time I went to a Reiki therapist and as she was pulling unsettled energy out of me, she said "something stubborn is attached to you and refuses to come off". Connection here?

Some attachments struggle and resist removal. Some of them swear, mumble, or smell as they come out. As I was in this dead of sleep, I recall hearing myself say, "oh no" ... and minutes later, non-stop belching (vomiting) volumes of air occurred. Coincidence? No.

Makes you wonder what else she (attachment expert) can do to a person from afar?

When my attachment removal experience was over, I recall my head falling back onto my pillow (bouncing a little) and resumed sleeping.

QUESTIONS/THOUGHTS

How did I feel the next day? Fine. Except I was very puzzled about my belching moment with my head bouncing back onto the pillow. Did I smell anything? Other than my breath? No. Did I recall swearing? No. Did I mumble? Yes ... the words, "oh no." Do I ever mumble in my sleep? All the time. Coincidence? No.

Some people asked me if I had felt more refreshed or in better health since the "clean out"? Not really. I was concerned my "lucky" attachment was now gone. Months later, I went to Las Vegas. I guess the expert did not get "all" of them as I won another jackpot. Or were the attachments on me not responsible for my "good luck" in winning jackpots to begin with?

Chapter 12
Fisherman Manifests on Boat

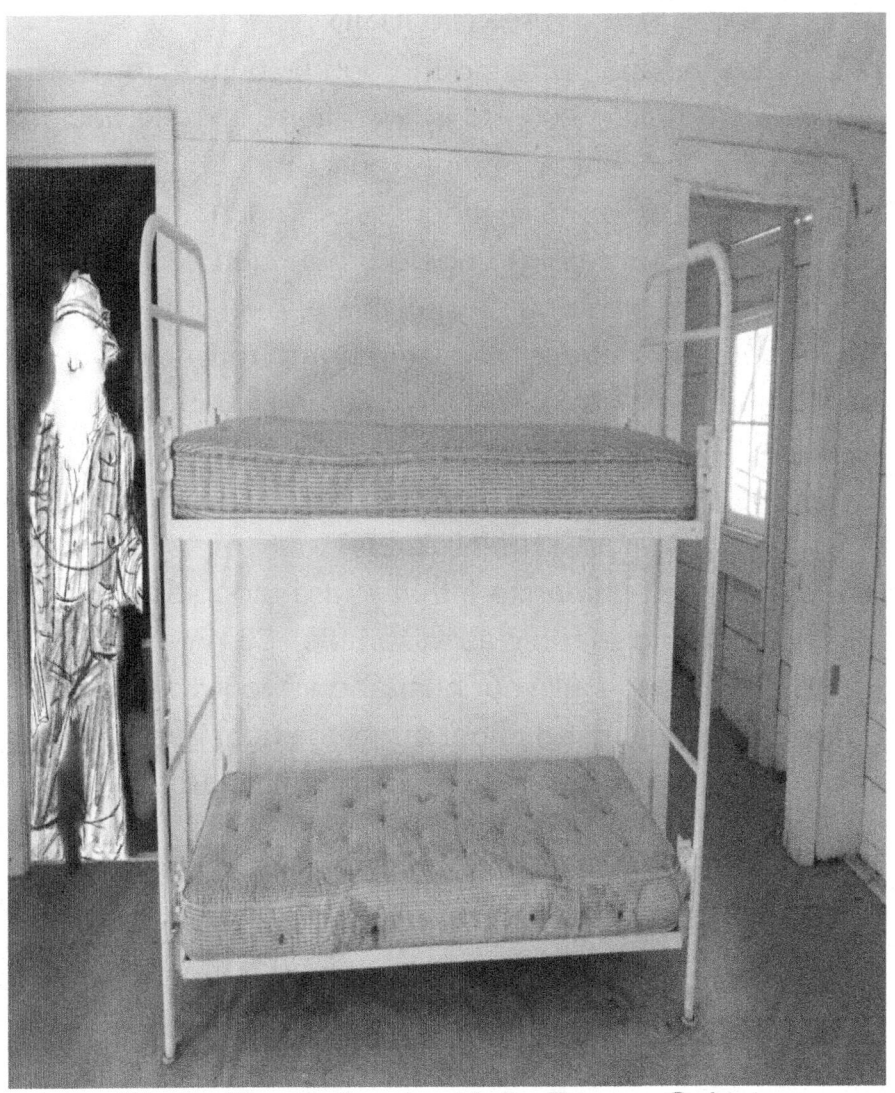

Photo-Illustration by Kelly Renee Schutz

Chapter 12
Fisherman Manifests on Boat

BACKGROUND

You are on vacation passing through Dubuque, Iowa with your husband. It is 2:00 PM in the afternoon. He decides he wants to stop at a marine museum. You have one stipulation ... to remain indoors as much as possible because it was hot out (temperature in high 90's F). Your husband jokes with you saying this is one of few places they have been that doesn't have paranormal activity. You tell him the paranormal is everywhere. He laughs at your comment. You go inside the museum building.

THE INCIDENT

You take the self-guided tour that ends outdoors. Being outside under no shade was miserable. Commenting on how hot it was, you tell your husband as you walk down a walkway, that you need to get out of the heat because you are about to pass out. He tells you to go ahead and to stand under a shaded area.

The shaded area is next to a couple of museum boats. He decides he wants to explore the first boat (empty) (no other people). You wait for him under a shaded awning. As the minutes are ticking away, you begin to wonder what is taking him so long. You feel heat stressed.

As you are about to go into the boat to ask him to hurry himself up, you see him popping his head out of the doorway looking in both directions. You think he is looking for you. You go to the door and walk inside the boat.

Your husband leads you to one of two rooms inside. You see nothing impressive. As you are standing in the bunk bedroom, your husband tells you (no one else is in the boat) that the boat is haunted.

You ignore his comment. You tell him it is hot out and that you need to get to the next building (cooler). He says nothing more. You tour the final building and go to your car.

While in the car preparing to leave, you ask him, "what makes you think the boat was haunted?" "It's blistering hot out." "Maybe you are just dehydrated."

Your husband (skeptic-believer) tells you while he was looking around in the bunk bedroom, out of the corner of his eye, he saw a man standing in a doorway. He thought it was just a tourist.

However, as he focused on the man, it was no more than 3-5 seconds when he disappeared right before his eyes. This was the point when he looked outside the boat to see if it was another tourist. No one in sight.

Because I was standing under an awning looking at the doorway to this boat, I can confirm no one else was around. Just the two of us. I did notice my husband looking out of the boat in both directions.

He described the man as being about 5'8 inches tall, no face, trim white beard close to face, tan shirt, tan pants, no shoes, no belt.

I asked him while in the car why he didn't impress upon me that he saw something paranormal. He told me I discounted his comment and wanted to get out of the boat to go to a cooler location. I asked him if he may have been hallucinating due to the heat. No.

My husband has been on this paranormal journey with me for a long time. He was at one time, a hard-core skeptic. To this day, he talks about the fisherman apparition he saw in the boat without my bringing it up.

DEFINITION

Apparition – a ghost or ghostlike image of a person. **Hallucination** – an experience involving the apparent perception of something not present. **Heat Stroke** – condition marked by fever and often by unconsciousness, caused by failure of body's temperature regulating mechanism when exposed to excessively high temperatures.

THOUGHTS

I see my husband evolving in his having paranormal experiences. Every time he mocks a ghost being near or tries to pretend something out there does not exist, he is proven wrong. I have witnessed this convincement by ghosts for years. I have seen my husband in a possession. I have seen him frozen into a trance in a haunted room. I am glad he had an encounter with a friendly apparition. I just wish I was there to have seen it. Apparitions generally show to one person. It is not clear if this ghost was residual or intelligent. And this was in broad daylight.

Chapter 13
Nanteos Mansion Country House

Illustration by George Patsouras
Nanteos Mansion Country House, Aberystwyth, Wales

Chapter 13
Nanteos Mansion Country House

BRIEF HISTORY

A very brief history of the Nanteos Mansion Country House is discussed in this chapter. A more extensive background of the property, its former occupants, and some hauntings can be purchased through Janet Joel (2015) at **jan.j@aol.co.uk**. **Website: www.nanteoshistory.co.uk**. The main focus of this chapter will be on its reported hauntings as well as my own experience that occurred in the Edda room the evening of May 28, 2016. The history, as reported below, is credited to Janet Joel, for her extensive work and research.

NANTEOS MANSION COUNTRY HOUSE

Nanteos Mansion Country House is a large, square, Georgian building surrounded by the beauty of the Welsh countryside. It lies in the Paith Valley, near Aberystwyth. The site has a long history of occupation that dates back to the 1600's. An earlier dwelling known as Neuadd Lawdden existed there for many centuries before Nanteos was built. The present mansion was built in 1739.

The earliest known inhabitant of the Nanteos estate was Colonel John Jones. He raised the Cardiganshire Militia in support of King Charles I during the Civil War. He had three daughters, Mary, Anne, and Elinor. Anne succeeded on her father's death in 1666.

Anne Jones of Nanteos married Cornelius Le Brun, who was born in Cologne, Germany. He came over to Wales to work in the lead and silver mines as a mining engineer. After making his fortune, he became High Sheriff of Cardiganshire in 1674. When he died in 1705, Nanteos was left to his only child, Averina (1675-1738). She married William Powell (1658-1738) of Llechwedd Dryrus, which was situated across the Paith Valley from Nanteos.

William and Averina Powell lived at Nanteos and had five children, Thomas, William, John, Anne, and Elizabeth. When William died in 1738, the estate was passed on to his eldest son, Thomas, who immediately began to build the present home at Nanteos. Before completion of the mansion and while attending Parliament, Thomas died of an apoplectic fit in a London street. He left no legitimate heir to his estate. He did have an illegitimate son who lived at Nanteos. This illegitimate son never acquired Nanteos.

Nanteos was left to Thomas' brother, The Reverend William Powell, who took over the estate in 1752. William carried on with the building of Nanteos completing it in the late 1750s. The lengthy history continues with its interesting twists and turns of ownership. Let's move onto the hauntings.

HAUNTINGS

The information that follows is credited to Janet Joel for her extensive detail and research in reporting the hauntings of the property. My own as well as current staff experiences will be added to this list toward the end.

SMALL DWELLING. Before Nanteos was built, a previous mansion was built on the site. Going back even further, a small dwelling was on the site with evidence of a large dark cellar underneath the property. Two windows, large front door, and thick walls are evidence of a previous dwelling. Anyone hanging around?

MONKS. In the dark, 60 foot long cellar, it is believed that seven monks lay buried. It is said that the seven monks came to Nanteos with the dissolution of the monasteries in 1539. With the Cistercian Abbey Strata Florida in danger, the monks fled to Nanteos for safety bringing with them a sacred relic which is reputed to be the Holy Grail.

HAUNTINGS ON THE GROUNDS

HARP, THE WOODS. On a still peaceful night, Gruffydd Evans can be heard playing his beloved harp deep in the Nanteos woods. Every year for 69 years, Gruffydd Evans would play his harp at Christmases in the music/salon room in the mansion. He was a relative of the family and lived to 92 years old. He is buried at Llanbadarn Fawr Church, near Aberystwyth.

BLACKED OUT WINDOW. On the west side of the mansion is a blacked out window. Originally, there were two windows blacked out, one on the ground floor and the other immediately above on the first floor. It is said that a member of the Powell family was returning from war, his wife and daughter were waiting for his return looking out each of the windows. As he approached the

driveway (on his horse), the horse became startled by a fox that ran across its path, the horse bolted, and the man fell to the ground breaking his neck. He died instantly. The two windows were blocked up immediately. The sign of a fox sitting on the lawn was a sure sign of an impending death in the Powell family.

MAN ON DRIVEWAY NEAR LAKE. A figure of a man can be seen on the driveway near the lake. He is seen waving his arms about looking as though he is herding animals or shaking off water. Some years ago, this man had been seen twice in a very short period of time. He is speculated to be David Rowlands, who drowned in the lake in 1899.

STABLE YARD. The stable yard at Nanteos has had numerous reports of hauntings for centuries. Unexplained horses and voices have been heard in the empty stable yard. In one situation, on two consecutive nights at about 4:00 AM, someone staying in the stables apartment heard raised voices and loud noises in the yard but as soon as he/she looked out the window, the noise abruptly stopped. A baby was heard crying in the stables apartment on a number of occasions. Horses in the stable yard have nervously reacted to something that the handler could not see.

SOBBING BOY. At a recent summer fete at Nanteos in 2014, a young man felt the presence of a young boy sobbing in the corner of the stable yard worried that he was going to get punished for something he had done. This spooked the young man as he had never experienced anything paranormal before.

BACK OF THE MANION. On another occasion, a horse and carriage was heard in the courtyard at the back of the mansion. Heavy footsteps were heard entering the back door and walked toward the kitchen dragging what sounded like heavy chains.

WILLIAM GRIFFITHS. A ghostly figure identified to be William Griffiths the Groom, who was killed by the Head Gardener (garden rake) on October 12, 1782, can occasionally be seen standing in the shrubbery, as if he is waiting for someone.

HAUNTINGS IN THE MANSION

There have been numerous ghost stories associated with the mansion over the past several years.

THE GREY LADY. The most well-known haunting is that of Elizabeth Owen, also known as The Grey Lady. Elizabeth Owen married Reverend William Powell in 1744. They had bequeathed Nanteos at the death of William's brother, Thomas Powell, in 1752, Elizabeth died at the completion of Nanteos in 1757.

Elizabeth's husband loved her so much that he showered her with jewels. She could not bear to be parted from her jewelry that just prior to her death, she rose from her deathbed and hid her jewels. Later that night, she died. She is said to haunt the corridors of Nanteos searching for them. She appears as a misty figure in a long, flowing gown. She wanders like a lost soul searching for her hidden jewels. Be warned – she will haunt anyone that dares to find her jewels.

CANDLESTICK IN 1930. During a party held at Nanteos one evening in 1930, the house was full of guests. An army officer went to dress for dinner. Ascending from the stairs to his room, he met a striking woman in an evening dress, holding a strange looking candlestick. Thinking she was one of the guests, he bowed and said "good evening" to her. The lady did not answer but carried down the stairs as if she had not seen him. He thought this was strange but continued up to his room. When he returned to the party, he gazed around for the lady. Eventually, he asked if anyone had seen her. Immediately, he was taken to the side and was told to never speak of the lady with the candlestick or there would be a death in the family. That night, Edward Powell died. A few weeks later, that same candlestick was found in a dusty top shelf corner of the silver vault, in the Butler's Pantry. Speculation that this ghostly haunt was that of Elizabeth Owen.

CHILD FALLS DOWNSTAIRS. A young girl read to Margaret Powell every evening at her bedside in the Macaw Room until very late in the evening. Edward Powell had warned the girl to leave at 11:30 PM, never to stay until or past midnight. One night, she did read over the specified time. Realizing this, she ran down the stairs. On her way down the stairs, to her disbelief, she saw a ghostly figure. It is believed this was The Grey Lady, Elizabeth Owen. The young girl screamed, fainted, and fell down the stairs hitting her head on the grandfather clock at the bottom.

Edward Powell was sleeping in Col. Powell's bedroom at the time when he had heard the commotion. He rushed to her. Checking that she was alright, he told her to never speak of the ghost she saw. She was confined to her bed for three weeks after the fall. She never spoke of the incident until many years later.

NURSERY – 1800s. In the 1800s, a young nursery maid, Mary, who had been working at Nanteos for six months, had to sleep in the Pink Dressing Room as the mistress of the house was sick in The Pink Room. One night, Mary was suddenly awakened by a figure leaning over her bed. She became so startled that she screamed. The figure then stood upright and walked straight through the closed door. Mary never slept in that room again.

TWO LADIES – 1920's. A similar occurrence happened to two American ladies staying at Nanteos in the 1920s. One stayed in the Pink Room and the other stayed in the Damask Room. After going upstairs to dress for dinner, there was a commotion. The lady in the Pink Room ran out and crossed the corridor carrying her belongings to her friend's room shouting, "I'm not gonna stay in THAT room," She never revealed why.

GHOSTLY MIST. A guest had thought he/she saw smoke in the inner hallway. In disbelief, the smoke mist transformed itself into a figure of a woman dressed in a long flowing dress. She began coming toward the front door. The guest was so stunned, he/she ran to Aberystwyth not looking back.

MID-1970's. A lighted candle had been left in the entrance hall window. The next morning, it was found in the upstairs bedroom with the flame blown out. How it got there, no one knows.

FURNITURE SOUNDS, EMPTY ROOM. Old houses have their creaks and noises. On occasion, furniture in a room located on the second floor is heard being dragged across the floor. When the room is known to be vacant and is investigated, it is found that no one has been in the room and the room is completely empty.

TILTING CHAIR. A tilting chair has been seen by a couple in one of their rooms. When approached, the chair will either fall back on its four legs or topple over.

SITTING ON BED. Sometimes, people sense a weight of someone sitting on their bed in a few of the bedrooms. At night, it may feel as though someone is tugging at your foot only to find nothing to cause that feeling.

OLD LAUNDRY ROOM. It had been reported that raised voices were heard coming from the Old Laundry Room. When investigated, no one was in the room. During an incident, it was found that four towels were piled very neatly in the center of the bathroom floor and a bar of soap had been carefully unwrapped from its wrapper and placed dead center on the bottom of the bath. No one claimed to have done this.

CROWDS OF PEOPLE, SOUNDS. A crowd of people had been heard by numerous guests at various times of day and night. One guest, thinking visitors were in the hallway, didn't question the incident until morning. Noises were heard around 3:45 AM. No one was in the hallway or visiting at this time of the morning.

HELLO, COOK. A young girl continues to be seen all over the mansion being spotted in various locations. One day, she (appeared to be 7-8 years old) had been seen running through the kitchen and said, "Hello, Cook" to the Chef. He gave chase to her and she disappeared. Two other members had seen a shadow of a small child in the kitchen area at different times. The only known recorded death of a child at Nanteos is that of Harriet Powell, daughter of William Thomas Rowland Powell, who died in 1857 (age 13), of consumption (known as tuberculosis).

Harriet Edwyna Powell (1844-1857)
Died of Consumption (known as Tuberculosis)

QUESTION ABOUT AGE AND APPEARANCE. It should be noted that IT IS possible for a child to LOOK younger than when they passed away. Two examples, the young child I photographed (see Chapter 4 - Faces in the Window in this book), was about 10 years old when she died [at a different location]. She appeared in the window as someone who looked to be 6-7 years old when I captured her image. In another example, a woman talked about her son. When he had died, he was much older than how he appeared in several pictures she had taken since. She was confused as to why he would show up in her pictures as a young looking 18 year old when he passed around the age of 24-28 years old.

MARBLES ROLLING. One night, the night porter was seated in the entrance hall and could hear marbles or pebbles rolling in the Inner Hall on the stone slab floor continuing to roll onto the wood floor going into the library. He checked the video cameras and could see nothing so he walked into the Inner Hall from the kitchen door hoping to catch a glimpse but saw no one. He turned on the lights and there was no evidence of any marbles or pebbles on the floor. Harriet has been known to take and hide marbles she likes. Some set marbles out in a bowl for her giving her choices.

DOGS COWER IN TRAINING. During the early 1990s, the mansion was empty but was managed by a caretaker. Permission was granted for the Fire Brigade and Police

Force to train in the empty mansion at regular intervals. The Police would train their dogs to retrieve hidden substances throughout the house, including the cellar. Police dogs are generally trained to deal with all kinds of dilemmas. When they entered the cellar door, the dogs began to cower and nervously whimper refusing to go into the cellar.

WILLIAM THOMAS ROWLAND POWELL. A young girl visiting the mansion in the 1970s was upset by seeing an angry man looking at her from the top of the stairs. Returning many years later, she remembered the incident and recognized the portrait of the man hanging on a wall.

William Thomas Rowland Powell (1815-1878)

TV CREW – STRANGE EXPERIENCES - EARLY 1980s. A newspaper reported ghostly goings on at Nanteos when a television company was making a production for a Welsh film company S4C. It was reported in the Western Mail that a two-day filming schedule was disrupted by "strange experiences" such as doors opening and closing on their own. A broken music box suddenly started to play. Movement of a heavy four-poster bed. A cloaked figure disrupted the shooting of several TV scenes. The crew refused to work after dark.

OTHER REPORTED HAUNTINGS BY STAFF

1. **Reported by Manager, Steven.** There was a wedding on the property a few years back with few children hanging about. A 3-year old boy tells his mother that he is going to go upstairs to play with a little girl. The little girl, most suspect, was that of Harriet Powell. As the 3-year old was making his way up the stairs, the mother grabs him and is visibly shaken because she knew no little girls were upstairs or at the wedding.

2. **Reported by Manager, Steven.** Steven was upstairs in one of the rooms. When he turned around to leave, the apparition of William Powell was standing in the doorway looking at him. He

saw his full figure. He becomes startled. Powell disappears. My ghost psychic expert predicted a former owner would be watching over the staff who ran the hotel making sure all remained in order.

3. **Reported by Manager, Steven**. Reports of the door slamming in William Powell's room. Feelings of being watched while he is in his room. Asks permission before entering Mr. Powell's and another (forgot name) rooms. Has seen glimpses of apparitions walking into various rooms in the mansion – will avoid those areas.

4. **Reported by Staff, Anna**, It was during the past year (would have been in 2015), when she was in the Morning Room, located on the main floor. She was hovering (otherwise known as vacuuming). Without warning, the door slammed and the lights went off. She said she saw a shadow figure either behind her or somewhere in the room. She explained to the unseen apparition that she was sorry but the room needed to be vacuumed. She turned the lights back on, opened the door, and continued until she was finished. "Something" doesn't like loud noises.

5. **Reported by Staff, Sien**. She reports and I witnessed the lights in the Inner Hall doorway continuously going "on and off" "on and off" "on and off" with no one passing through the door.

There is a motion sensor hard wired within the doorway. It had been checked by an electrician who says it is in proper working order with no known defects.

I stood and watched the light go "on and off" continuously the evening of our stay and also noticed that it rarely went off in the daylight (day after). I shot video of this occurrence.

6. **Reported by Staff, Sien and Anna**. A portrait of son, William Edward George Pryse Wynne Powell (1899-1918) hangs in the sitting area in the Entrance Hall in front of the reception desk.

   A feature light hangs above the portrait and MUST be left on 24 hours a day, otherwise, the "entity" gets upset and starts knocking on the wall. KNOCK KNOCK.

7. William Edward Powell was the only son of William Powell (picture on previous pages) who was killed in action during the First World War on November 6, 1918.

   He is buried in Maubeuge Centre Cemetery in France. Who is pounding on the wall? William Powell? As a tribute to his son? See image below.

William Edward George Pryse Wynne Powell
Died in Battle/War at the Age of 19 Years

SIDE NOTE ABOUT PAINTINGS: I have found that in many of the historical homes I stay in, that most of the paintings on the walls are from garage sales and are not "anyone" who use to reside in the home.

Most of the original paintings in the Powell home were sold years ago. Few original paintings exist in the mansion. Paintings on the wall are relatives, friends, or others demonstrating the period. According to the manager, items that use to reside in the home are now finding their way back.

MY EXPERIENCE IN EDDA SUITE

When we arrived to Nanteos, we were not certain which room we would be staying in for the evening. Staff member, Sien, was kind enough to show us to our room, located in a building attached to the side of the mansion home. At first I felt a little disappointed. It had been reported that few hauntings occurred in this room.

William Powell's room could be seen from our window. The Edda Suite, located in the new addition, was built where the BAKERY use to be.

I always knew that if a place was haunted, the "ghosts" would come and find me. And, "something" did. We did not leave empty handed during our stay there. I managed to capture something in the Morning Room and of course, the Edda Suite.

OUR EVENING IN EDDA SUITE
OCCURRENCE 1:30-1:45 AM

Art Illustration by Brandy Woods
EDDA Suite, Nanteos Mansion Country House

PARANORMAL OCCURRENCE. My husband and I were in the Morning Room in the main mansion house from 10:00 PM until around 1:15 AM. We were alone with no others around us. He was reading a book and I was using my computer. I set out a few trigger objects (pink and blue rubber duckies) directly in front of me as seen in the picture below. I had my K2 meter on with full battery power. When I get hits on my K2 meter above 4 bubbles (with no other means of affecting the metering, like a cell phone, I know I have captured something paranormal). This meter is showing 5 bubbles. Something was intrigued and visited.

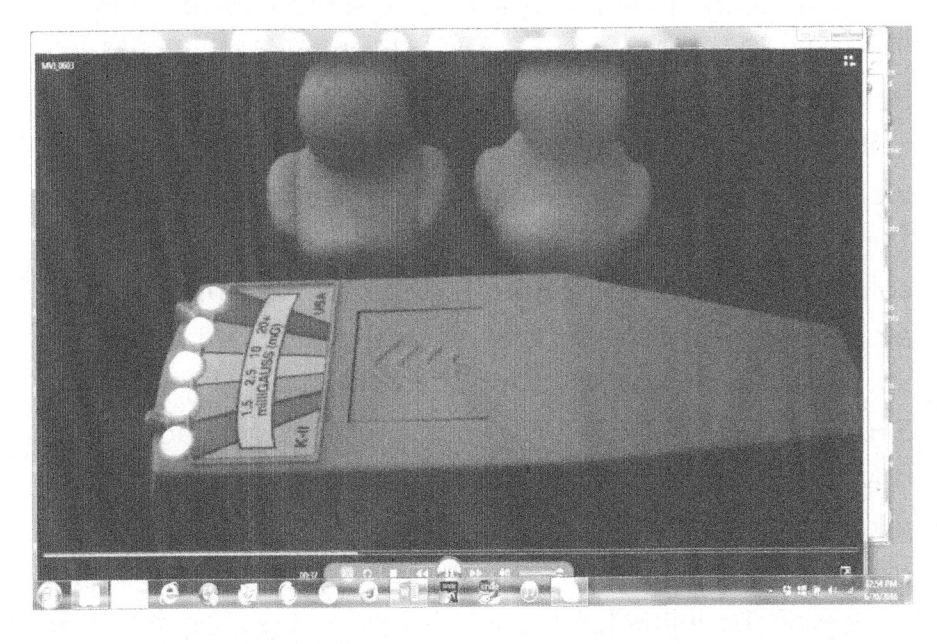

This is suggestive of paranormal activity. Manager, Steven and staff member Anna, came in around 11:30 PM to check on us. Steven and I chatted for nearly 2 hours.

When they left, we decided to call it a night. As we walked through the Entrance Hall (main reception area), I stopped to look at the portrait that needed its light to be on 24 hours a day. I then looked at the Inner Hallway, where that sensor light continuously went "on and off." I took video of it.

FEELING WATCHED. As we were making our way out of the main building, we walked down the stone hallway (flooring not level) and out the back door. As we were walking the short distance to the next building (new addition where bakery use to be), I stopped and looked inside the Old Kitchen window, where tables were set up for bed and breakfast guests. We both felt as if we were being watched. This made me pick up the pace a little faster to get to the door that led into the building where we were staying. We walked up several stairs to get to our Suite. When we walked into the EDDA Suite, my husband said he was feeling watched. I didn't feel anything but the air in the room didn't necessarily feel right.

SHATTERED NERVES. Within 20 minutes, we had lied down to go to bed. My husband falls asleep quickly. It takes me about 15 minutes on a good day. A little disappointed we weren't staying in a haunted room, I had turned off the lights for the first time in 3 days [my previous 3 nights were at 3 other haunted hotels].

BED SHAKING. "Ahhhh," I said. Just before I was about to sleep, I suddenly felt the bed shaking and bouncing. Thinking it was my husband's feet, I initially ignored it.

FOOTSTEPS COMING NEAR ME. I then felt footsteps walking all over the bottom of the bed. I could feel every individual step. It felt to me like an anxious child or dog fumbling around. It was at the point when I felt the footsteps walking up the center of the bed (between my husband and myself) that I said out loud, "NOT AGAIN" ... and started smacking my husband's arm asking him "WHAT ARE YOU DOING OVER THERE?"

HUSBAND SNORING. I knew my husband was asleep (snoring). Upon my outburst, the sensation went away. I told him when he woke up that something was on our bed. As usual, that was met with temporary puzzlement followed by a loud snore.

WHO OR WHAT WAS THAT? The question is ... WHO or WHAT was walking on top of me on our bed? WHO or WHAT was walking down the CENTER of the bed toward my face? It felt to me like a curious dog cautiously making its way toward me.

Or was this a CHILD that wanted to lie down between us?

CHILD AND DOG WHISPER'ER. I have known for years that I attract the following: (1) children, (2) dogs, and (3) ghosts. It didn't surprise me if our visitor on our bed was either. Who was in the Morning Room with us? Not sure. Did this entity follow us back to our room? Not sure. My ghost psychic (expert) told me that the entity came through our window that had a vase in front of it. Confirmed. See image.

However, it is hard to determine WHAT was on us because the sensation felt as though it could have been either (child's feet or dogs feet). Felt like dog feet to me. How do I explain the bouncing or shaking of the bed? I can't.

The arrow pointing to the window (as you look out) is that of William Powell's room in the main mansion (haunted). See below. The other arrow below that, is the vase that was in front of the window.

OTHER REPORTS IN EDDA ROOM. The only other report we were informed of (the next day) was by **Chris**, a staff person, who we ran into on our way out of the building. I had asked him if he was aware of any other occurrences in that room. He said the only other one he was aware of was when some guests were staying in that room and "something" slammed the door and then opened it again. I am speculating he was referring to the BATHROOM door. The main door into the room is very heavy and would have been a challenge for a ghost.

DOGS BURIED ON PROPERTY. In review of the history, there are over 80+ dogs and xx number of animals buried on the Powell property, including the pet cemetery. In 1865, in a registry entitled Nanteos Harriers, the Powell's had listed over 80+ hounds, all named with the beginning letter of "P." We had visited the pet cemetery that day and took note of several tombstones. As Janet Joel writes, "originally, the kennels were located on the front lawn, close to the turnpike road. The hounds were then relocated to new kennels due to the damp marsh land on which the kennels were built. The dampness had caused ill health of the pack. The new kennels were then relocated on the east side of the mansion in 1870." It is uncertain how close this structure was to our room. All pets were loved and buried on the property. Do ghosts of animals exist? Yes, they do.

SAD STORY - JACK THE COON. In attempting to locate information on Jack the Coon, I couldn't find any. Who was this man? "Jack the Coon" means ... Jack, who was a Negro or African American.

Jack worked on the Nanteos property (date unknown) and was a faithful employee. He gave tirelessly of his time and energy. He was a kind person. When he passed away, the local cemeteries refused to bury him or any African American in their plots.

Out of respect for Jack, the Powell family buried him amongst their 23+ beloved dogs and pets in the Pet Cemetery.

When his wife, Jenny, not sure of her skin color, passed away, she refused to be buried anywhere else except right next to him. The pet's cemetery can be seen surrounding a holly tree and the oldest mulberry tree in Britain.

Photo Taken by Kelly Renee Schutz
Pet Cemetery

Poor Jack the Coon and Jenny (Wife)
Nanteos Mansion Country House, Aberystwyth,
Wales

Tales of Apparitions #3

Chapter 14
Children of Deadwillow Manor

Photo Illustration by Magdalena Adic
Tales of Apparitions

Chapter 14
Children of Deadwillow Manor

Several years ago, my husband and I decided we wanted to stay at a bed and breakfast somewhere in Canada. In my searching the Internet for possibilities, I came across a place located just outside of Toronto named *Deadwillow Manor.*

I cannot tell you what intrigued me about this property. I would imagine it had something to do with the word *dead* in its name. Since I am a ghost seeker, how much more interesting could this experience be than to start with a name that gave a person the shivers? When I read the advertisement about the property, it said nothing about it being haunted. In fact, this was of no surprise since many inns are cautious about revealing their haunted histories for fear of losing clientele.

We arrived to *Deadwillow Manor* on June 14, 2009. Our plans were to stay there for three days. As we drove onto the property, we noticed few trees and shrubs surrounding the manor. I didn't see any "willow" trees either. My first comment to my husband was, "*certainly looks a little dead around here.*" I began to ponder how they may have selected their name.

Behind the building was a rustling stream that glistened when the sun's rays hit its moving peaks. If anything, I felt I could at least sit in front of it admiring its rushing waters as there is nothing more calming than being around water.

As we dragged our luggage out of the car, I stopped for a moment to smell the clean air. Coming from a large city where there is always smog alerts, it made me appreciate opportunities like these when you can breathe clean air. The temperature outside was a cool 56 degrees with few clouds drifting across the sky. Light breeze. We proceeded to go inside to check in at registration.

As we entered the building, what struck me quickly were all of the antiques strategically placed in rooms on the main level floor. One could not help but notice two items in the sitting room that were displayed prominently – a doll and a truck. I knew there must have been a story behind each of them as they appeared to me to be taking center stage within the room.

As we walked up the stairs to our bedroom, I felt as though I was not walking those steps alone. Although my husband was ahead of me, I had an odd feeling that someone was walking right next to me. Long drives and feeling tired can play tricks on a person's mind. As we approached the door to our room, I looked around the hallway and noticed a few pictures hanging on the wall.

One picture was that of a young girl and the other was of a young boy. My thoughts turned to the toys in the sitting room. I began to wonder if these pictures had a connection to them. As we entered our room, the décor was basic looking with the feeling of an unimpressive hotel room.

Around 6:30 PM, my husband and I went down to the manor's onsite restaurant to eat dinner. As we walked down the stairs, we cut through the sitting room area to gain entrance to the restaurant. While cutting through, I had noticed the doll and reached for it trying to touch it. The owner notices me doing this and says, "Please don't touch that doll. She doesn't like it when her doll is touched."

I am now feeling startled and bewildered and comment, "may I ask, who is she?" She replies, "the little girl who lives here." "Little girl?" I mumble. "I wasn't going to lift it up, I just wanted to touch its clothing since it appears to be rather aged," I comment. "Please don't touch the doll," says the owner.

It was at this point that my comfort level went from a 10 to a 2. My feeling unnerved was just the beginning of our evening. We sat down at our table and began to review the menu. As I looked around me, I noticed that we were the only two in the room. As the owner walked by me I said, "small crowd tonight?" She replies, "small crowd every night. What can I get you to drink?"

When the owner left the room, I looked at my husband and said, "mistake being here. I don't think we are alone." "Don't talk like that," he says. I commented back, "something about that doll sets a little girl off. Who is this girl? I feel a presence walking with me up the stairs and the owner acts overly protective. What are we dealing with here? A demon child?" Husband replies, "nonsense."

The owner then comes back and gives us our drinks and takes our orders. I take the opportunity to ask her, "May I ask you a question? Who is the little girl?" The owner replies, "the little girl's name is Ella. She died on this property with her brother, Jordan, years ago when they drowned in the stream just behind this building. On occasion, they like to hang around. As long as you do not touch their things, they won't bother you."

U-WEEE-U-WEEE-U-WEEE-U. I felt like I was living a nightmare on an episode of the *Twilight Zone*. Creepy woman, ghost children, don't sneeze or someone might get offended. I turned to my husband and said, "I guess that means we shouldn't touch the doll or the truck." "Let's just eat," he says.

As we finished our meal, we decided not to look around the main floor and proceeded back to our room. As we were getting near the stairs, a marble rolls and bounces all the way down the steps nearly hitting me. I grabbed it as it made its final bounce. We both looked up the stairs awaiting another marble, but nothing else came hurling down. I said to my husband, "you go first."

As we were getting ready for bed, I could sense a presence in the room. So I said, "Ella, is that you?" No reaction. "Or is that you, Jordan?" No reaction. "We are both happy to be spending our night with you on your lovely property. May we ask for some peace now so we might go to bed?" No reaction.

The evening remained rather calm. Being a believer in moon phases, I had checked the moon before getting into bed. The moon was nearly three-quarters full. I felt that the energy field wasn't strong enough to elicit strong activity in the room.

The next morning, my husband noticed that his shaving cream was missing from the sink area. I told him to check his suitcase. As he opened its lid, he noticed that shaving cream had been sprayed all over his clothes. I had asked him if he thought he took it out of his bag but forgot to and it accidentally malfunctioned releasing the contents. He said, "no, I brought it to the bathroom and set it down on the counter. I have no idea how it got back into my bag and why it's all over my clothes." It was at this point that I swore I heard a *giggle* in the corner. I asked, "are you in this room with us little children?" No reaction. "We were told not to touch your things, so please do not touch ours." *Giggle.* Faintly heard.

It was at this point that we decided to change our plans and forego the additional two nights. We decided a refund for the remaining nights was not worth our asking and we left the property.

As we drove away, I looked back at the window to the room where we had stayed. The curtain was moving but no one could be seen. I told my husband to speed up and get out of there.

GHOST CHILDREN

Most ghost children are playful and are not harmful. However, depending on the circumstances surrounding their death, one should never assume a ghost child is friendly unless you are assured their energy is friendly. On occasion, my husband and I encounter two ghost children who visit us from across the road [former farmstead]. They were killed by their father with an ax during the Civil War era. No one knows for certain why he snapped but he also killed his wife in the same manner.

When our ghost children visit us, they make it known that they are around (mischievous). Sometimes, I want to raise my voice to them and scold them for hiding or moving my things. One should not raise your voice to any ghost (child-teen-adult-elder) unless you understand the type of energy it possesses. In this story, we were warned about the little girl not liking her doll to be touched. This felt demonic to me. Shaving cream in the suitcase? This felt harmless, but mischievous. Best option was to leave the property.

Chapter 15
Deceased Shape-Shifts Into Body

Illustration by Halida Dwi Edyati

Chapter 15
Deceased Shape-Shifts Into Body

BACKGROUND

Most of us are raised to believe when we pass away that our soul (energy) goes directly to heaven or to a higher place. Some of us are taught to believe when we die, someone we recognize (or not) will greet us and bring us to the pearly gate to meet God, a higher power, or to our loved ones.

I know a few people who are atheist and do not believe in a place of rest after death. They feel when the lights go out, life as we know it is over.

INTERVIEWS

Over the years, I have chatted with people who have passed away suddenly but came back to continue their life journey on earth. Not all saw the tunnel of light. Not all saw a beautiful sky with green grass and flowers. Not all believed in God. Some saw a light tunnel. Others saw nothing but darkness.

PERSONAL STRUGGLE

During November 2020, I came down with a bad case of COVID, I nearly passed away twice (at home). There was no hospital bed for me (filled with patients) and even if

189

there was, the last thing I wanted was to be incubated. My husband, who was also suffering from COVID (lesser), stood by my side 24/7. He refused to let me die. He rounded up all the Catholics he could find to pray for me. I also prayed - silently and in darkness.

There came a point where I was losing my battle with COVID. People were telling me to "fight," How can you fight against something you cannot see. How can your body defend itself against something so powerful that it continues to ravage your body with its destruction?

There came a point when I thought the end was near. During this time, I felt at peace but saw only darkness. I was told then by some that the reason why I didn't see a tunnel of light was because it wasn't my time to go. And, only then, would I see a hand reach out for me to help guide me toward a brilliant glow. I saw darkness.

BELIEFS IN THE AFTERLIFE

We all have our beliefs as to where me might go after we pass away. Some truly believe when lights go out, its over. I don't believe this because I have seen too much evidence while doing paranormal work to suggest otherwise.

I hope someday, if Heaven is real, I will see nothing but beautiful bright vivid colors. I hope to be reunited with relatives and pets, I once loved. I hope to meet those I have wondered about for years (my distance relatives). I hope to be around positive energies I can laugh with and feel at peace with. Those are my post-life dreams.

THE PASSING

My father passed away in December 2016. During this time, I was teaching at a college 600 miles away. They had a rule for instructors to not miss class. I knew my father had passed when the movie screen in my classroom began slowly (with control) rising. I had no idea this was happening until my students alerted me to it.

I stood there and watched it slowly rise. I knew right then and there that my dad had passed away. There was nothing I could do. I couldn't even break down and cry. I couldn't run out of the room. I couldn't get into my car and start driving up to Minnesota. I had to stand there in front of a full classroom and finish my lecture.

ANGELS

Do angels alert you when your times become tough? Some do. I knew my father would come see me at some point. I felt guilty for not being with him on his final day.

Or was this his final day?

THE INCIDENT

My father never wanted to die. He fought to stay alive. In a brief conversation with him one day, he expressed to me how frustrated he was about his years being cut short. He said to me, "is this it? Is this all life is giving me?"

What he was trying to say was that he felt cheated out of more years of his life. He lost his battle to kidney failure and colon cancer.

THE MOMENT

All of my family members were alerted my father was passing away, except me. One by one, they all arrived at hospice to say their final goodbyes. My goodbye would be at his wake.

I lived in Indiana at the time (600 miles away). I was teaching in my classroom when my father left life. It was at the point when my movie screen began rising (slowly) that caused a panic with my students (pointing frantically) and my realization that my father passed.

THE LOBBY

However, as each of my family members said their last goodbyes and proceeded to the lobby to await my father's final moment ... my younger brother went over and stood by a window-glass door. It was seconds after my father passed that something strange occurred.

My younger brother told me there was an elderly man sitting in a wheelchair in the lobby. He was slumped over with his chin down to his lap.

At the point my father passed away, the elderly man lifted his head off his lap and eagerly started to wave in his direction. It was as if he wanted to alert my brother of something. Something so odd that it raises questions about life after death.

My brother looked at the elderly man. As soon as the waving stopped, the elderly man slumped back into the same position he was in before my father passed.

THEORIES

THEORY #1 - The elderly man was smiling and waving. A moment of unusual energy. It was as if my father's departing energy had flown right into him. It was his way of saying, "I'm not gone, I am in this man's body."

THEORY #2 – The elderly man had seen my father's energy (soul) departing and was giving him a "wave" send off as his soul was flying out of the glass window-door. They say the veil is thin as you near death. Perhaps this man didn't make it much longer also being in hospice.

THEORY #3 – The elderly man realized other people were around him and just decided to wave. Given the circumstances, seems a bit odd though not ruled out.

DEFINITIONS

Death – the end of the life of a person or organism.
Energy – the strength and vitality required for sustained physical or mental activity. **Shape Shifter** – a person or being with the ability to change their physical form at will.
Transfiguration – a complete change of form or appearance into a more beautiful or spiritual state.

QUESTIONS-THOUGHTS

My father passed away peacefully with family members by his side. My sense of guilt living so far away and not knowing his end date is something I will never get over.

My father did come to visit me in Indiana three months later. He attempted to call me on the phone (yes, that is right) AND his farm smell, that I recognized, engulfed me by surprise while I was working on a project at my kitchen table.

Even though my father wanted to cheat life and live longer – there is the possibility that he demonstrated something most may not be aware of ... the ability to go into another person's body to attempt to live.

MEDICAL DOCTOR

I spoke to a medical doctor (on my podcast show) and asked him if it were possible for the deceased (energy) to shape shift into a live human being (post-death).

He told me during his practice as a doctor, he experienced and was aware of three cases. So, yes, it is possible.

However, the question remains ... how long can energy from a deceased person (post-death) remain in a live person's body?

We will never know that answer.

Chapter 16
Neurodivergent Beacon

Illustration by Magdalena Adic

Chapter 16
Neurodivergent Beacon

BACKGROUND

For the past several years, I have been on a mission to identify and uncover where I have acquired my ESP (extra sensory perception) abilities from.

I was perfectly happy accepting the fact that I may be a Starseed child (Indigo). However, that perception of me is beginning to change since my reading about neurodivergent disorders.

Although I fit every general characteristic a Starseed may have, what I do not believe is that I was sent to this planet from another to advance the thinking of our human race.

Or am I?

After all, I do podcast worldwide. My shows are highly ranked. My voice is perhaps trusted. Do I offer what the world is seeking right now? Is the world ready to hear about the unusual, odd, creepy, and bizarre that life is showing me? Maybe I am a Starseed ... or ... do my ESP capabilities come from another place? I wrote this article to be published in a magazine. I will publish it in my book first.

ARTICLE

Extra Sensory Perception Abilities Awaken Sixth Sense
Am I A Neurodivergent Beacon?

THERAPISTS OFFICE

Therapist: *Why do you think unexplained situations happen around you?*

Me: *I don't know.*

Therapist: *Let's go back in time to when you were a child. Do you ever recall having moments when you noticed stuff happening that made no sense?*

Me: *That's a vague statement. Young kids don't analyze their world at that age. They just live it. How far back do you want me to go?*

Therapist: *As far back as you can remember.*

Me: *Well, there was a time when I was age 4. I recall having visions of traumatic events that would show on television the next day. At first, I passed them off as a coincidence. As they happened more frequently, I felt I was causing them.*

Therapist: *What were some of your visions?*

Me: *Airplane crashes, war situations, assassinations, drownings. Negative.*

Therapist: *How did these visions come to you?*

Me: *In my mind. A quick visual flash. Sometimes in my dreams.*

Therapist: *And these visions happened around the age of 4?*

Me: *Yes. I would say they continued until about age 9.*

Therapist: *Do you recall experiencing trauma as a child?*

Me*: Depends on your definition of trauma. Yes. When I was three years old, I experienced a sad, devastating event. A death. I do not want to talk about it.*

Therapist*: Do you continue to experience visions?*

Me: *Yes. And they remain negative. They seem to appear to me as warnings about people wanting to target me. Problem is, I can never stop these situations from happening.*

Therapist: *Interesting. When having these visions, what mental state are you in?*

Me: *Depressed or extremely tired.*

Therapist: *Has your depression ever been treated with medication?*

Me*: Only for a short period of time. I don't like taking pills. I don't believe in masking something not completely understood. Maybe my brain is wired differently.*

People ask me if I am psychic. *Maybe.* They ask me at what age did my extra sensory abilities begin to detect unusual happenings? *Age 3-4.* People ask me if I believe in ghosts? *I do.* People ask me in what ways have I experienced the supernatural? *I have been able to sense, see, feel, hear, and smell what I cannot explain. Maybe my experiences simply come from my mind.*

Questions

Is there a reasonable explanation as to how extra sensory perception (ESP) abilities develop in the brain? The research on this has been inconclusive. Based on numerous studies, neuroscientists believe ESP does not exist because findings cannot be replicated in controlled conditions.

Expanding on this question further, could there be a relationship between neurodivergent brain disorder and ESP abilities as they pertain to the experiencing of paranormal encounters? This is an interesting question.

Preliminary Perspectives

Neurodivergent brain dysfunction is described as a disorder or disability that affects the way a person receives and processes information. Examples of disorders might include autism, dyslexia, trauma, developmental disabilities, ODD, OCD, ADD, PSTD, ADHD, anxiety, gifted, epilepsy, auditory processing, and other specific learning disabilities. In looking back at my therapy session, I was diagnosed with anxiety and depression but was never tested for dyslexia, ADHD, or ADD.

Extra sensory perception is described as impressions the brain receives or communication that occurs without involvement of any of our communicating sensory organs. Extra sensory phenomena generally fall into three classified categories: (1) precognition (knowledge of future events), (2) clairvoyance (awareness of future events and outcomes), and (3) telepathy (ability to know thoughts of people separated by distance). Other examples might include: (4) clairaudience (ability to hear messages) and (5) clairsentience (ability to sense energy). In my younger years, it was apparent to me I experienced all categories.

Brain Function

Brain function and health are unique to every individual. Comprised of two hemispheres within the brain (left and right), the left (logical) and right (creative) serve as bases for other connective lobes that perform specific functions. If either hemisphere of the brain is injured or overstimulated, this could affect regular functioning resulting in electrical pulses that misfire, go astray, or change areas in the brain while in a corrective state.

Lying directly in the middle of the brain is the pineal gland. The pineal gland is vital for physical, mental, and spiritual health. It serves as the gateway to higher consciousness, spiritual awakening, and psychic abilities. If the pineal gland were compensating for an injury, it could electrically overstimulate either area within the brain that open to what we call our "third eye" or "sixth sense." There remains a lot to be learned about brain function.

Younger Years

I saw the psychologist when I was age 17. I decided it was time for me to get help in ridding my depression and anxiety. I lived a life always in constant turmoil. I learned to push my anger, anxiety, and emotions deep inside me. As a result of years holding my emotions inside, I developed an ulcer.

The first line of treatment as prescribed by the psychologist was for me to undergo hypnosis to calm my anxiety. When I told him I needed help with the visions, he discounted them as being mere coincidences. The visions worsened.

Connecting The Dots

At the age of 3, I recall experiencing my first traumatic event (death of a family member). I also recall around the age of 5, falling down a tall flight of stairs hitting my head against a concrete floor. By the age of 6, I found myself struggling to remain focused in school, couldn't figure out homework, had no attention span (especially when reading boring books), was sensitive to behaviors and the acts of others, and turned to isolation to escape emotional pain. On the flip side of the coin, I found myself to be incredibly observational as compared to others. Around the age 9, I found myself experiencing clairaudience (grandparent's house, chatter in the kitchen, no one in there, in house alone). Around age 14, I wanted to see a ghost on my father's childhood property and inadvertently manifested two apparitions there several years later.

By age 17, I fell into a severe depression. What I learned later in life was that my participating in hypnotic sessions triggered within me a deeper depressive mental state activating premonitions, psychic predictions, and remote viewing abilities. By the age of 20, a psychic warned me my mind was very powerful and to calm my anger issues. Around age 30, I was physically attacked by something I could not see in my grandparent's home in an upper floor bedroom. In my 40's, as mentioned earlier, I photographed two apparitions in a screened window that telepathically spoke to me. By the age of 55, I haunted three homes, observed my husband under a possession, experienced a few trance situations, moved objects with my mind, was choked by, sat on, and kicked up into the air by an unseen energy, dealt with poltergeist activity, and noticed a blood red handprint on my chest that remained for 3 hours (elongated fingers, crooked finger). To this day, I still do not know if that handprint was spiritual, paranormal, or extraterrestrial. I only know it wasn't mine.

Now age 60, I have encountered more than 100+ paranormal situations and 3-4 perceived extraterrestrial visitations. Like a beacon, I do not need to search for ghosts anymore. They come searching for me. I may never know whether these occurrences stemmed from my brain function (mind) or if there is a paranormal explanation.

Reactions to Sensing Energy

The living, deceased, and children can sense my ESP abilities and react accordingly. For example, deceased energies appear to be drawn to me as if I were a beacon of light. Their mission seems to be wanting attention or communication. The living appears to sense my abilities and refer to me as highly intuitive and empathic. Their desire in wanting my attention is to vent to me openly about their personal issues. Children and pets alike are highly sensitive and insightful beings. Both seem to seek from me time, attention, and sensitivity.

Children and ESP

Some theorists believe when babies are born, they enter this world with brain functioning that starts at the same place ... a clean slate. However, these theories do not seem to explain how some children (usually under the age of 5) demonstrate exceptional gifts such as knowledge of historical events, unique perceptions, vocal and musical talents, or ability to predict futuristic outcomes.

What is even more impressive is when young children, usually under age 5, share details about their past lives, known as reincarnation. If babies begin life with a clean brain-functioning slate, then, how can we explain past life memories and being gifted without years of development or training?

One observation is clear, as the child ages, the desensitization process of ESP abilities appears to block sensory perceptions and are replaced with influential attitudes based on environment, religious affiliations, parental opinions, distractions (school), and refocus (sports activities).

With the suppression of conscious awakenings, ESP abilities go onto the back burner until a later time in life when something unexpected or unexplained challenges the logical and creative hemispheres of the brain. For example, let's presume a person is experiencing what appears to be a paranormal incident. Studies have shown when a person encounters an unusual situation they cannot critically explain, the right hemisphere of the brain activates their ESP abilities attempting to justify the situation. However, most left (logical) brain functioning individuals remain skeptic regardless.

Parapsychology, ESP, and Psychological Disorders

Some parapsychologists believe the existence of ESP abilities is caused by certain types of brain activity not necessarily associated with neurodivergent disorder. Brain activity can change or become restructured over time due to injury, overstimulation, or correction by electrical pulses (rewiring within the brain). For example, a person who is struck by lightning, electrocuted, or hit in the head may suddenly find they have ESP abilities in predicting the future. However, having an overactive or compensating pineal gland can also act like an antenna (beacon, light) drawing unexplained perceived paranormal experiences. Why this occurs, no one knows.

We ask the question if those who experience ESP abilities are more intelligent. No. Having psychic or extra sensory perception abilities do not equate to having a higher intellect. Knowing the outcome of a futuristic event is not considered a measure of intelligence.

ESP abilities may also develop from situations that involve (not limited) - epigenetic transmission of parental genes (trauma), environmental influences, religious beliefs, traumatic events, complex or typical PTSD, near death experiences, or by having a brain function disorder-disability known as neurodiversity.

Neurodivergent Disorders

Someone who may have a neurodivergent disorder might be described as a person whose brain functions differently in one or more ways as compared to standard or typical learning measurements. Neurodivergence, however, can manifest in different ways and at different points in life. People who are classified as being neurodivergent can demonstrate this disorder in a mild or severe form. Those having a mild form may go unnoticed while others with severe forms behave differently than the norm as established by society (known as neurotypical).

As stated earlier, some examples of neurodiversity are: (1) autism, (2) dyslexia, (3) trauma, (4) complex PTSD and/or typical PTSD), (5) developmental disabilities, (6) learning disabilities, (7) ADHD, (8) anxiety, (9) OCD, (10) auditory processing, (11) sensory integration disorder, (12) gifted, (13) developmental co-ordination disorder, (14) ADD, (15) Tourette's, and (16) epilepsy.

Back in time, it was not a common practice in my school to test children for disorders. First, not enough information was known about disorders. Second, there was a consensus that children should not be labeled with a disorder as this would excuse common mental development issues. And third, as one ages, one might experience a health issue resulting in altered brain functioning. For example, someone who develops epilepsy may experience brain changes but not necessarily acquire ESP abilities. On the flip side, ESP abilities are not necessarily altered by having a neurodivergent disorder. As the brain attempts to compensate for injury, it is likely ESP abilities could be hindered or heightened but not guaranteed.

Walking Our Path to Understanding

We all walk a unique path in life and leave our footprint. No two footsteps on the same path leave the same mark. For years, I have been searching for answers on *how* my ESP abilities and mild neurodivergent disorder(s) have opened my sixth sense allowing me to experience unexplained "perceived" paranormal situations. Like a puzzle nearly finished, I realize I may never find that one missing piece that explains the connections of my abilities.

Always Grateful …

Dr. Kelly Renee Schutz

ABOUT THE AUTHOR

Dr. Kelly Renee Schutz is the host-producer of the highly ranked podcast, Paranormal Encounters Podcast Series. She is an open-minded sensitive-intuitive-empath who has earned five degrees in human ecology, management, communications, education, and paralegal litigation in law.

Aside from a long list of interests, she is a speaker, author, artistic creator, voice artist, and storyteller of personally experienced paranormal and extraterrestrial experiences. Dr. Schutz has an interest in parapsychology, ufology, consciousness, and life-after-death issues.

She has experienced 100+ paranormal encounters and 3-4 extraterrestrial visitations since the age of 9 affording her opportunities to self-publish ten, working on eleven books in her Paranormal Encounters book series. She has been featured on several radio and podcast shows, author-blog-book sites, two-page magazine spread in Writer's Life Magazine, has produced a 22-segment CD called "Maynard and Mildred", and will be featured as a workshop speaker at the 4th Annual UFO Mega Conference (2023), booth vendor and presenter at the 2nd Annual MN ParaUnity Convention (September 2022), and booth vendor at the Metaphysical and Paranormal Expo, Janesville, Wisconsin (April 2022).

Visit her official website at www.paranormaluniversalpress.com to learn more about her, upcoming appearances, or write her at krschutz1@yahoo.com.

Tales of Apparitions #4

Chapter 17
Haunting on Bezzle Lake

Photo Illustration by Kelly Renee Schutz
Tales of Apparitions

Chapter 17
Haunting on Bezzle Lake

"Where are we? I think we are lost. It feels as though we are out in the sticks," I said to my husband as we were driving to our destination. "I think we are okay," says he. "What does the GPS say?" I asked. "It says we have three miles to go and then to turn right at the next road," husband comments. *Driving.* "Turn here," he says. "There it is - wow – what a beautiful lake!" I said.

Bezzle Lake was like no other we had ever seen before. It was situated in the middle of a dense grove of trees just off of a low traveled, two-lane road in the middle of nowhere. We would not have known about this lake if it were not for my winning a get-away package at a silent auction we participated in held at an art gallery I showcase my work at near Chicago. It was obvious to both my husband and myself that upon our arrival to the lake that very few people camped there.

As we approached our turn and drove down a long, grassy road, as directed by our GPS, we noticed a rough, one-lane, weedy road taking us into a very isolated parking area that didn't accommodate more than three vehicles. As we got out of our car, I looked around and what struck me the most was how calm *Bezzle Lake* appeared as it beamed with a feeling of peacefulness.

"Ahhhhh … peace and quiet for a weekend," I said. As I walked closer to the dock, I noticed a canoe was hitched to it giving the impression that someone else may have been visiting the area.

"Who do you think this canoe belongs to?" I mumbled. "I have no idea," says my husband. "What does the brochure say we get for our winning this spectacular weekend get-away?" I said.

"It says that we can pitch our tent in the commons area just to the left, use the grill at our own risk, and use the canoe to explore the lake," he replies. "Are you kidding me? This is all we get? Are you telling me that this canoe is part of the package and it doesn't belong to anyone? Who-hoooo," I said as I beamed with an adventurous spirit. "Let's make the most of it," husband comments.

So, here we are. Two people standing next to a peaceful, glass smooth lake in an isolated area on a weekend get-away filled with adventure. The lake not only provided us with a sense of calmness but gave us both the feeling that we were stranded on our own little island. "Our own little island," I said. "Yes, well, let's not get overly excited about that," says my husband.

Not use to the feeling of isolation, we turned on our car radio, sang out loud, unpacked our things, and pitched our tent.

"Why do you think few know about this place?" I said. "Probably private property and don't want riff raff camping here," husband says. "Good point," I mumbled. "Let's start exploring the lake before it gets dark," husband says. "Do you know how to navigate a canoe?" I expressed with concern. "I know enough to get us around the lake, soooo, let's jump in and go," he says. "Should I bring anything?" I asked. "Bring a few waters, we'll be back before dark," husband expresses.

As we pushed the canoe away from the dock onto the smooth lake, we began to paddle ourselves down the middle of it. As we moved further away from our campsite, the image of it began to dissolve into scenery that surrounded it.

"Let's not go out so far. This makes me feel nervous," I said. "In fact, maybe we should go back before we get lost," I nervously mumbled. "Relax, enjoy our short vacation in nowhere land," husband says. "It is not every day that we are able to explore like this in a place we have complete freedom," he proclaimed.

As we glided our paddles through the smooth water, we would on occasion feel as though we were hitting something moving. "What was that?" I said. "It is nothing more than our paddles bumping into some fish who are feeding on the surface," he replies. "What time do you have?" I asked. "Six-o'clock," husband comments.

"Why does it get dark here so early?" I said. "Ooops! We better head back, the time here is actually one hour ahead, it is really Seven-o'clock," he says. "Oh God, it will be dark soon, let's get moving," I expressed with nervousness.

As we turned the canoe around, we noticed the lake looked stretched out on all sides widening in every direction. It felt as though we were in the middle of an ocean. As we looked around for something familiar, nothing appeared to jump out to help navigate us back to our camp. In fact, we knew we were lost on the lake.

With no people around us, no homes, no other camp sites, and no objects or lights to help us navigate back, we soon realized we would not be making it back to our camp before it became pitch dark. "What direction is our camp?" as I paddled with fear in my voice. "Straight ahead, I think," husband mumbles. "Hand me a flashlight," husband asks. "I didn't bring one," I said. "You said we would be back before dark," I mumbled. As darkness fell quickly upon us, we found ourselves stranded in the middle of the lake.   211

"Let's stop right here and not go any further, I am afraid we might topple over if we keep moving," my husband says. "Oh God, we are going to die on this lake?" I said. "Just relax and remain still," he said. "I'm starting to get cold," I said.

As we positioned ourselves in the canoe to secure its movement, we swatted mosquitoes and nestled close together for warmth. It felt as though hours had turned into days as we awaited morning. Then, the conditions around us began to change. "What was that?!!" I expressed with fear. "It sounds like wildlife crying in the woods," husband says. "I think nocturnal animals are rustling through the weeds or bats are making themselves known in the moonlight." I express with anxiousness. "I hate this," I said.

"What was that?" I stated again. "Nothing, go to sleep," says my husband. "I think something is in our boat with us," I nervously commented. "Go to sleep, your imagination is running wild," he says. It was at this point when our boat started to rock side to side. "What was that?" my husband says. "The boat is moving?" I said.

"I have no idea, it is very still out here so what could be causing it to move?" he nervously replies. R-O-C-K .... R-O-C-K ... R-O-C-K. "WHAT IS GOING ON!?" I scream. "I don't know, I can't see anything. I can't tell what is rocking the boat," he says. "Make it stop!" I beg my husband. "How can I make it stop when I can't figure out what is causing the boat to rock back and forth?!" he says.

A cold breeze rubbed up against my face and my leg is touched. "I don't have time for getting cozy!"

I said to my husband. "I am over here, I can't even reach your leg," he says. OH GOD …. !! (Mutual).

Chapter 18
Energies That Attract Ghosts

Illustration by Brandy Woods

Chapter 18
Energies That Attract Ghosts

ENERGY. What is energy? According to Live Science (2014), energy can exist in a variety of forms, such as electrical, mechanical, chemical, thermal, nuclear, and kinetic.[2,3] Energy can be transformed from one form to another.[1,2,3] Human emotion, for example, especially if it is negative emotion, is a form and source that not only attracts angry ghosts but is what they feed off of in order to manifest.[1]

Ghosts usually make their presence during times when a person is most unaware or unable to visually see them is not always hanging around to absorb their energy. People who strongly wish or are overly zealous in wanting to see a ghost rarely have an experience because their anxiousness acts as a blocking mechanism affecting their sensitivity. Most people think a ghost will appear in a visible form, often recognized by facial and body features. These manifestations are the most difficult to achieve in the spirit world because if they do occur, they can only manifest (show) for about 3-5 seconds before fading away. Many of these situations also require the right conditions to manifest such as weather, type of conductor (stone, metal), energy source (lightning, energy field, emotion), moon phase, and personality of the seeker.[2,3]

How do you know when a ghost is near you? A combination of cues are usually presented to indicate a presence. For example, temperature changes (ice cold), smells, tingling, touch, feeling extremely ill, dizzy, faint, or drained, low energy, arm hair stands on end, equipment malfunctions, feeling an electromagnetic field around you, and unexplained movement, tampering, or sounds of objects. Kinsey (2013) suggests situations in which a ghost may be present:[4]

1. If a candle suddenly burns blue, a ghost may be present.

2. If a candle suddenly extinguishes where there is no draft or other cause, a ghost may be near.

3. If you suddenly smell perfume or cologne (smell that reminds you of your loved one), he/she may be checking on you.

4. If you look into a mirror that belonged to a dead person, your loved one might be looking back at you (esp. if they looked into the mirror before dying).

5. If a rocking chair rocks by itself (with no other explanation), you may have a ghost in your presence.

6. If dry kindling wood won't light, a ghost may be blowing out its fire.

7. If you smell fresh dirt or rotting wood (with no source), this may be the smell of a ghost out of a grave.

8. If the hair on your arms stand on end for no good reason, you may have a ghost present.

TERRITORIAL. Are ghosts that hang around specific locations territorial? Some can be territorial. It has been my experience that the personality of the deceased and their sense of attachment to a location can determine the type of haunting one might experience when investigating situations. Not all ghosts are nice. Not all ghosts are mean. Some ghosts (few) are demonic. I do need to caution you that most authentic experiences involving the presence of a ghost requires a combination of cues in order to bring about its validity. Before any situation can be declared as being paranormal, the conditions of the location must be evaluated and debunked (as to their causes – see last chapter in this book) with your searching for the most obvious explanations of what appears to be usual first.

PRIVACY AFTER DEATH. Why should we care if something is living in our home and affected by our presence? After all, it is OUR home. This may be true but not always when it involves a territorial spirit. I had asked this question years ago when my husband and I discovered that we were living in a haunted home. What started out to be a peaceful ghost had suddenly turned into an aggressive ghost. At first, the energy in the home felt peaceful. I didn't think much of it. That was until one day the energy started changing and unusual events began appearing to be more aggressive. Our peaceful ghost was attracting other entities into your home, perhaps through a portal we later discovered in our livingroom.

Although you may consider yourself to be a happy person, living a happy life, in a happy family, and believe to be living in a peaceful environment, your assumptions that the nice ghost you have in your home will be at peace with your existence may be further from the truth. Does this mean that you should move? Not necessarily. Assess your situation before acting. Read the next section entitled, "Apparition Attractors."

As an example, in watching an episode of a haunted television series called, *The Haunting*, a happy family moved into their dream home only to discover a demonic energy resided there. In trying to be at peace with this entity, backlash occurred by the demonic energy who wanted the home all to itself. The demonic energy did not care how peaceful this family was and went to extremes to scare them out of the house. Angry or demonic energies, especially, who remain here on our earth can be aggressively territorial often guarding their space and privacy.

My hobby in investigating haunted situations is exploratory – one of fascination. It became personal when my relatives showed in the window screen. It became a hobby when I began seeking other locations known to be haunted to search for the truth. It became interesting when apparitions made their presence known to me allowing me to discover their potential energies. It will become a retired hobby when it becomes too dangerous for me.

Many of us have heard the phrases, "focus on the here and now" **or** "Don't dwell on the past, look only to the future." When you become a ghost hunting enthusiast, like myself, being able to determine if those who have passed still hang around and for what reason, creates a mindset of fascination opening up a dialogue about the mystery of what happens after we die. Are we alone on this earth? I believe the answer is, "no." Be careful what you wish for ....

Apparition Attractors

According to an article written by Manchester Paranormal Investigations (2016), there are reasons why someone's home may experience paranormal activity.[1]

First and foremost, there may be residual energy left from a previous resident who may have been highly disturbed (severe depression or anger) or experienced a traumatic event causing extreme negativity to remain and be absorbed into objects or walls. Apparitions with pleasant personalities or character do hang around. However, their energy is not usually strong enough to attach to objects or walls. What is it about negative emotions that are strong enough to attach to things? I am not sure.

Second, there may be an intelligent spirit who chose not to move on or is trapped because of an anchor holding it to this realm. In life and death, some souls do not want to depart and remain protective over property, objects, and places meaningful to them.

Third, the most difficult entity to remove from a location is one who is attracted to a person's negative energy feeding off of it.

Finally, from my own personal experience in living with ghosts, I have an open attitude about them and because of this, they like to hang around me. Ghosts who visit me do not always live in my home. Ghosts can take up residence in any home or location they feel comfortable in coming from a radius of 1-2 miles away in any direction from their place of death. Some people might debate distance as being further. The environment they seek could be one of peace, comfort, familiarity, or highly charged negativity.

I am aware of situations where family feuds have occurred over the ownership of property often not ending in death. In some cases, the former siblings (deceased) will return to their childhood home or place of location to reclaim what they felt they were cheated out of. This assumption is hard to prove but often speculated by family members if "unrest" appears to plague a property. In most situations, 99% of spirits that hang around are peaceful and non-interactive; however, 1%, if provoked, may stir up a cycle of bad luck, aggressiveness, or simply being a pest.

HUMAN EMOTION. According to an article written by Manchester Paranormal Investigations (2016), what attracts negative entities to you or to a location is human emotion.[1] Examples of negative emotions (constant) are anger, bitterness, fear, frustration, guilt, jealousy, regret, self-doubt, and sorrow. Everyone experiences negative emotions from time to time, it's a natural part of living. However, having this feeling every day can attract negative spirits to feed off of this energy. Why negative energy and not positive energy? I cannot answer this question.

Actions such as yelling, fighting, arguments, and rebelliousness feed negative entities. Most people experience stress from their jobs, have up and down marriages, encounter financial troubles, and succumb to health concerns. Negative energies want unhappy people to remain unhappy so they can use that energy against them so they can gain more energetic power in hanging around causing personal chaos and destruction.

Sound a little far-fetched? Perhaps. Negative energy cycles lead nowhere but back to themselves. I have experienced these types of continuous cycles where nothing but bad luck always circled back to me – coincidence? Perhaps. Was there a negative ghost or demon hanging all over me? Not sure. I needed to blame something [negative attitude] for my bad coincidences. How does one break the cycle of negativity? It is not easy but through the practice of positive thinking.

UNHAPPY HOUSEHOLDS. Do unhappy households attract negative energies? Sometimes. Negativity is a highly charged emotion. Highly charged emotions can embed themselves into walls, stone, or other objects within the environment. You have heard of the phrase, "if walls could talk." Have you ever noticed that people who move into a different home may remove some of their walls if they sense energy in the home doesn't feel right? The best way to remove a negative entity from the environment is to try and REMOVE THEIR ENERGY SOURCE. This is not always achievable.

QUESTIONS AND THOUGHTS

Have you ever walked into a room or building and said, "the air in this room feels heavy or uncomfortable." Some people feel it and others do not. Why? String of bad luck incidents do not always equate to having a mean spirit hanging around you. However, ask

yourself this question, when you do have bad luck experiences, how do you turn those moments into something positive?   If we set aside human emotion for a minute and look to other reasons for possible energy attraction, what might they be?

SITUATION TYPES. According to Manchester Paranormal Investigators (2016), there are four types of attractions for negative entities. They are:[1]

1. **Attracted to an individual**. Negative inhuman entities can target an individual if they sense one's psyche is not strong enough to fend off attacks. For

example, those suffering from severe depression, specific types of anxieties, and illness are candidates for attracting negative entities into their homes. Because I have experienced this in my own homes, I tend to agree with this assumption.

2. **Attracted to the environment**. Common, negative entities are attracted to a particular location due to the energy available to them. They find a suitable habitat and they thrive off of the environment. They can also cause some havoc just to increase the emotions in which they feed from. In some cases, certain types of building materials can also pull energy into the walls creating a breeding ground for activity. Because I have experienced this in my own homes, I tend to agree with this assumption.

3. **Pool of negative energy**. If a location has a history in which there were very strong emotions in the past, the location can be ripe for negative entities. Energies are absorbed into the structure. It can range from the residence of a former prisoner to a house where one member lived with mental illness or a debilitating progressive disease such as Alzheimer's or dementia.

4. **Invitation (unintentional or intentional).** Through the use of divine practices (Ouija board) or even amateur EVP sessions, entities can be unintentionally invited into a location. The entities can sense that someone is willing to communicate with the spirit world and they use that opening to invade your space. Even attempts using this board by a previous resident can cause problems for new owners. Locations in which there were darker intentions (rituals), where evil has been invited in are especially problematic and can be for many years. The advice about Ouija boards is to not play with them as it is difficult to rid negative entities once they have manifested into a location.

MY CHILDHOOD / PERSONAL DEMON. When I was a child, I used to go to bed at night and pray that the disturbing noises created in my head would stop. For each and every day of my young life, I would pray that I would have happy days rather than miserable ones. Over time, these noises started affecting my health, self-esteem, nervous system, and mental state of mind causing me to believe that my purpose in life was to simply suffer. How does one know if what he/she is experiencing is really a growing physical or mental health change rather than some entity affecting them? This is a difficult question to answer.

On many occasions, during what I felt were some of my darkest hours, I would fall asleep and see a demon laughing in my head. Where did this demon come from? Some would say I was having a hormonal imbalance causing me to experience this vision.

Though I agree this could be possible, I also know that what I was experiencing seemed to never end and felt very real. This demon would taunt me, mock me, and crush what little confidence I had in myself. I would go to school trying to be positive only to come home feeling depressed, hopeless, and worthless – often experiencing a sense of isolation and disconnect from the world.

Eventually, these continuous setbacks would turn into a string of bad luck for me where it was like a self-fulfilling prophecy. I always expected to have a bad day ... I always expected to not be liked ... I always expected to feel like an outsider. I hated coping with my anxieties and struggles.

Some would say these feelings are common when growing up as a teenager. However, to me, these feelings were not common enough when I watched people around me appear happier, livelier, and more willing to live. I really felt something negative was watching my every move and hanging all over me.

There came a point where I wanted to see if I could turn my internal suffering into something positive. One method I used involved the art of distraction. With limited resources to keep me entertained at home, my process began with writing to several pen-pals from around the world who I felt would not judge me (this worked on my self-esteem). When I needed to come out of my shell more, I would play music and sing (this worked on my being introverted). When I wanted to express my inner creativity more, I would work on my 4-H projects. When I needed a physical release, I played on a softball team (this worked to release tension).

Reframing my mind (negative to positive) would take years. However, getting to the root of the problem would come to light when I began interacting with new faces at college. Up until then, I was the perfect candidate for negative attraction.

Growing pains. It is normal to experience let downs in life. It is normal to feel depressed from time to time. It is normal to experience jealousy, hate, bitterness, and sadness. Our personal definition of "happiness" is not the same as someone else's. Being miserable or happy often roots itself into our emotions. Our expectations of ourselves can bring us down. Having setbacks makes us stronger and wiser. The way we grow and learn from our life lessons may not be the most ideal. It is when the anger or depression take over that we begin to lose focus, sabotage our dreams, and draw to us the wrong types of "energies" – i.e., demons, negative entities, negative people, etc.

Surrounding yourself with people who appear to be on the right track (personally defined), share a similar connection, or bring to you a sense of assuredness can deter negative energies from wanting to be around you. Why? Because your energy is what these energies feed off of. Who are these negative energies and where do they come from? They come from everywhere.

Focus on what is meaningful to you in your life while accepting disappointment as being natural. Rid negative people who bring your spirit down. Focus on your goals and what is important to you.

QUESTIONS AND THOUGHTS

Does this mean that if I am happy that I will NOT attract negative entities into my life? NOPE.

Natural Absorbing Energies

Human emotion is one source of energy that can attract unwanted energies into a home.[1] According to Before It's News (2013), there are also other types of energy attractors:[1] (1) types of home wiring, (2) materials used in the construction of basement, (3) compounds in the earth, (4) Feng Shui and layout of room(s), (5) amount of deaths or trauma in a location, (6) mental illness, (7) infrasound, solar, and geomagnetic storms, (8) physiology, and (9) personal beliefs.[1] These factors affect the environment and in turn, the environment can affect us.

FACTORS. Many factors need to be taken into consideration before pondering the idea if a location is susceptible for energy attraction.[1]

1. Use of Feng Shui. Described as "a system of laws considered to govern spatial arrangement and orientation in relation to the flow of energy, and whose favorable or unfavorable effects are taken into account when designing buildings." Strong energies or activity might congregate.

2. The trauma history of people who have died (civil wars) or experienced extreme mental or physical suffering in a location might show hot spots for hauntings.

3. The geology of the earth or where the construction of a building might be situated may tell someone if the location is susceptible for energy attraction.

4. The emotional or physical condition of people investigating the location can also have an effect, as overly depressed or angry emotions can act as "triggers" for creating imbalance.

GEOLOGY/COPPER/QUARTZ/SPRINGS/LEYLINES.[1]

WIRING. Copper wiring appears to be made of compounds strong enough to absorb energy.

STONE. Although limestone and granite are also found in haunted locations (strong conductors), it has been found that copper and quartz are more potent to drawing and absorbing energy.

WATER. Theories about the potency of churning water, such as rotations in springs and waterways, are often reported near haunted locations.

ENERGY FIELDS. Leylines, otherwise known as energy lines, are reported lines of energy running through the earth often believed to be power centers or source of vortexes. Also, moon phases.

STORMS. Geometric storms, especially those that contain lightening, produce high voltages of energy and when this energy strikes the earth that may be an energy source (absorber), such as limestone, the energy intensifies to a point where possible manifestation of ghostly images or activities occur.

CHECKLIST FOR HAUNTINGS

The following is a list of SOME energy absorbers that can aid in manifestations at haunted sites:[1]

GEOLOGY and CONSTRUCTION – most potent stone in order:
(1) Limestone, (2) Shale, (3) Sandstone, and (4) Granite.

WATERWAYS – if the site is within 1 mile of running water, stream, river, swamp, or ocean.

TRAINS – not significant to hauntings; however, people build their homes near train stations and trains tend to be built near towns and towns tend to be built near water.

EMOTIONS /DEATH/TRAUMA – negative emotions, sudden death (murder, suicide, accident); trauma such as severe depression leading to emotional imbalance, shock, anger, continuous hostility.

STRUCTURES OLDER THAN 50 YEARS. Research has not been clear enough as to why structures (buildings, homes) over the age of 50 years are candidates for being haunted. It is assumed that over time, especially in homes with dysfunctional families and those experiencing traumatic events, that energies accumulate collecting in walls (wiring, types of materials) or objects.

CONSTRUCTION. Masonry, block, and brick foundations can be energy absorbers. It is least likely to find objects (not structures) created from these elements in smaller amounts becoming haunted.

For example, the concrete poured where a sign might be placed is not usually in a confined area. Tombstones in a cemetery (as they are spread out and of small size) do not often absorb enough energy to manifest hauntings.

QUESTIONS AND THOUGHTS

Natural sources that absorb energy may explain how unexplained phenomena find ways to manifesting into various forms. What is unclear is how these absorption energies allow for unexplained entities to transmit sounds, form sounds into voices, or be able to intelligently throw objects.

What is also not clear is how these types of energy absorbers aid in the creation and sustainment of orbs and vortexes. Especially orbs that travel above, beneath, or are confined in portals. How do orbs get from one place to another beneath the earth? How are portals formed? What makes portals perfect transport systems?

Finally, we know that certain types of decomposition and gases create and release bubbles into the air (photographed as orbs). What is not known is whether these "decomposition or gas orbs" have similar mass compositions inside and whether they appear to be solid, translucent, patterned, or with a color.

Chapter 19
Types of Hauntings and Ghosts

Illustration by George Patsouras
234

Chapter 19
Types of Hauntings and Ghosts

You look at the outside of a house that has a unique architectural design. If it's a modern look, you probably don't think it is haunted. If it is an older home, your mind may believe it to be haunted. I have stayed overnight in older homes and have lived in newer homes. Both types of aged buildings have been haunted.

Many people have reported seeing, hearing, or feeling the presence of other worldly spirits, but not necessarily in their own homes. Some people believe ghosts are angels. Others believe ghosts are evil. So, who is right? Various researchers have different interpretations of what is considered to be "a haunting" as well as what constitutes a "type of ghost." In an article written by Kinsey (2013), she suggests six types of haunting activities:[1]

1. **Residual** – Technically not considered a haunting (non-intelligent), this type of ghostly activity refers to situations where deceased have left a residue of themselves, such as footsteps, laughter, crying, apparitions, etc. often from a single event (tragic, happy, or stressful) that repeats over and over. Sometimes the experience occurs during the exact time of day or if a trigger sets it off.

2. **Interactive** – An interactive ghost is considered to have a form of intelligence. It can see us, hear us, and communicate with us.

3. **Poltergeist** – A type of ghost often referred to as a "noisy ghost" said to be caused not by apparitions but rather by the human brain. It is speculated that the ghostly activity is most often linked to homes with females 25 years and under where deep emotions cause the poltergeist activity to become more powerful. I cannot agree with this definition entirely as the majority of my experiences with ghosts have occurred in my homes after I turned the age of 50.

   Poltergeists can initiate a haunting in a home that may involve phantom footsteps, unexplained cold spots, electrical problems, disappearance of items, foul odors, strange rapping, popping or scratching noises, movement of furniture, scribbles that no one will admit to, and voices or animal sounds,

4. **Demons** – Known as evil entities possessing negative energy, they are often up to no good and cause destruction. Sometimes, demons disguise themselves to be friendly with their main intention to weaken their target. Demons are not common but can occur, especially if playing the Ouija board, in a location where there was a history of negativity.

5. **Shadow Figures** – Ghostly images that may appear as shadows in a human shape or animal form. It is difficult to know if these apparitions are nice or evil. Shadow people have been seen in nursing homes wandering into rooms prior to a person's death. You may have heard of the phrase, "the shadow of death is upon him." Shadow figures have also been seen in many types of locations not limited to historical sites, churches, castles, and on battle fields.

6. **Portal Hauntings** – A portal is considered to be a doorway into another dimension outside our physical world that is considered an access point for the entrance of ghostly activity. Some researchers believe portals can be located above or below ground. Ghostly entities may be that of spirits of people who have lived before, or they could be something else altogether coming into our world for the first time.

Hauntings can occur just about anywhere on our planet. The type of haunting taking place inside or outside a structure is usually determined by several factors (environmental, history, trauma, and confusion or attachment by the entity). The environmental conditions are amplified further by the absorption of energy with the aid of earthly compounds or man-made materials such as copper, stone, or metal.

The balance within the system can be affected or triggered further by external factors such as human emotion, energy fields, and weather conditions. How entities come to be formed and what they actually are remain a mystery.

Levels of Ghost Hauntings

According to Kinsey (2013), she suggests there are five different levels of ghost hauntings[1]:

1. **Level One** – A haunting by a very weak ghost giving off sounds such as footsteps, physical sensations, feeling of cold spots, or smell of faint odors. Typical of an anniversary ghost, these entities have a tendency to repeat an action at the same time of day, week, or year (continuous loop) but for brief periods of time. This type of haunting is different from a residual haunting, often considered an impression.

2. **Level Two** – This haunting produces the exact same activities as a Level One ghost with the exception that the activity is louder and holds itself for a longer period of time. Activities might include laughter, talking, and an occasional brushing-by-feeling indirectly aimed at someone. These are non-interactive ghosts. They do not communicate directly with or respond to humans.

3. **Level Three** – This ghost is more active than a Level Two ghost. These ghosts express the same activities as Level One except this ghost can open doors and move objects. It may or may not have an interaction with their target. It may be considered an intelligent ghost that is aware of its target.

4. **Level Four** – This type of ghost may be seen visually. It makes appearances, usually in the form of mists, plasma, or a vague shadow figure. It interacts with humans and is aware of their presence. It can move objects, touch, make noises, and can create laughter. This type of ghost has the intelligence to interact with humans.

5. **Level Five** – This ghost can manifest itself into an ectoplasmic mist, become a moving orb, or show in physical appearance. As a physical form, it can be seen visually for about 3-5 seconds, often with the use of proper equipment. It may be fully interactive with a target and has intelligence. This type of ghost may communicate with its target by seeking help, may want to warn you, want you out of his/her house, or may be content to do as it pleases. These entities are usually visible, create sounds, move about, and tamper with objects.

Imprint?

COULD YOUR GHOST BE AN IMPRINT? Is your ghost just an imprint stuck in continuous cycle making its appearances during specific periods in time or by triggers?

An imprint is commonly known as "energy" that is absorbed into a specific location such as a floor board, wall, stone, astral plane (unseen dimension such as within the air), metal, etc.

According to Kinsey (2013), there are six types of imprints:[1]

1. **Imprint or Impression** – Something that is heard or seen that is "stuck" in a specific location. When a situation is triggered, something might manifest and start to replay. For example, you hear laughter in a room, go to investigate, and you find no signs of people or activities. Was this an imprint of people who use to gather in this location from the past? Another example is schools. Children's voices are often heard playing in specific areas. Is this an imprint of souls triggered by something replaying from their past?

2. **Historical** – A type of ghost that does not interact but can be seen. This ghost may be wearing period clothing and is always seen in that same clothing. May repeat actions regularly and can be seen in places enacting various scenes from the past.

3. **Crisis Ghosts** – The ghosts usually appear to a family or friend within the first week after death, then, disappear.

4. **Anniversary Ghost** – These ghosts appear at a certain time of day, week, month, or year. Repeats the same action. It may happen once or several times before vanishing. For example, you see a ghostly figure visiting a grave or landmark every week on the same day. They may present flowers and then fade away.

5. **Personal or Family Ghost** – These ghosts are attached to a family or certain member of the family. No matter where you move, the ghost will follow. Sometimes a ghost may appear during certain occasions (such as weddings) or you may smell perfume of that person before something is about to happen (such as hearing a door or floor creak).

6. **Haunted Objects** – Be careful what you purchase at estate or garage sales as you may be bringing someone home with you. Some deceased have strong attachments to certain objects. They may make their presence known by showing in your mirror, moving an object, playing with your music box, rummaging through your dresser drawers, etc.

Signs & Symptoms of Hauntings

SIGNS AND SYMPTOMS OF A HAUNTING. According to Kinsey (2013), as well as my own experiences, I agree there are signs and symptoms indicating you MAY have a haunting in your home:[1]

1. **Noises** – Always be sure that what you are hearing and noticing is <u>unusual</u> and not typical of house settling noises. For example, creaking floors, banging on walls, rivets popping from the shingles on the roof, etc.

2. **Missing or Relocated Objects** – Missing or misplaced an object? True story. My small leather neck pouch went missing. I had put it on a flat shelf near my computer. I

went to the kitchen to get something to eat. When I returned to my office to get my neck pouch, it was gone. I thought I was losing my mind. I went back to the kitchen in search of it. I told my husband (who had been in the livingroom the entire time while I was at my computer) that it was missing. He went to my office and found it hidden underneath my chair with the neck string just barely showing to capture his attention. How did my pouch get under my chair?

3. **Doors, Windows, Locks** – Do your doors, windows, and locks indicate a presence of something? Do you know if air drafts and the settling of the home foundation affects the opening and closing of your doors, windows, and cabinets? What about your locks?

   EXAMPLE. True incidents. One day, the air in our sitting room felt heavier than usual. This feeling was felt during a full moon phase. Over the past months, it had been noticed that during different moon phases, the hands on our dead clock located in our sitting room would move to different times. On this day, I stood in front of the dead clock, watched its hands move in front of me, made a comment about having a presence in our house, The next morning, the KEY that is in the lock in our front door had turned from a 12:00 position to a 10:00 position. My husband and I live alone and never go out this door. On April 18, 2016, the key was turned to a 1:00 position. Who or what is turning this key?

4. **Electronics and Electricity** – Also considered as gadget disturbance, you may notice unusual static in your landline phone, your TV and radio turning on and off by themselves, your microwave turning on without warning. Your lights flicker when there is no electrical issue. Your flashlights, watches, battery clocks, etc. go dead continually. What or who is draining the batteries in these items?

5. **Animals** – Dogs are ghost-haters and cats are ghost-lovers. A cat cannot always be predictable when it puffs up and gets skiddish. Does this mean that there is a ghost present? Not always. A cat may be attracted to a certain room. A dog, however, is very sensitive and may not like certain rooms often barking at what appears to be nothing. FYI - dogs, in particular, have very good hearing and can pick up sounds from a long distance (as far as 1-2 miles away).

6. **Sensation** – When was the last time you stopped for a moment to ponder that something didn't seem quite right in your surroundings? For example, atypical rush of air, cold or warm spots, feeling of

walking into an electromagnetic field, emotional and behavior changes, or strange touches. Have you ever found yourself wanting to quarrel with your loved one(s) more often than usual and for no apparent reason?

Illustration Mixed Media by Kelly Renee Schutz

Chapter 20
Moon Phases and Energy Fields

Do Ghosts Only Manifest During Moon Phases?

Photo Illustration by Kelly Renee Schutz

Chapter 20
Moon Phases and Energy Fields

This will be a short chapter. I will tell you what I know about moon phases and energy fields and how I have captured some of the most interesting apparitions, ghosts, entities during these periods of time.

MOON PHASES
Although paranormal activity can be active during periods when there is not a new or full moon, I have found that the most active hauntings I have occurred have been during CLEAR NIGHTS on new moon (three days before, during, and after) or full moon (three days before, during, and after) skies. It is not uncommon to experience a haunting during any other time when weather conditions are right - such as electrical thunderstorms, where the air is highly charged (allows for manifestations).

CLEAR EVENING SKIES / CALM AIR
Evenings where the sky is "crystal clear" and the "wind" is calm gives me the best results when capturing authentic entities. A clear sky allows for a strong energy field to reach the ground.

MANIFESTATIONS
Although most visible manifestations do not last for more

than 3-5 seconds, it is not uncommon to see orbs in motion remaining visible for more than 5+ minutes before vanishing into "thin air."

Actual Photo by Brandy Woods
Not Manipulated – Discovered 1 Year Later
Taken in the Morning from A Distance
Cowboy in the Window

Chapter 21
One Thump or Two

Photo Taken by Kelly Renee Schutz
True Story

Bed and Breakfast
Macdonald Norwood Hall Hotel, Aberdeen, Scotland
(May 2015)

Chapter 21
One Thump or Two

PHENOMENA

The love affair. After years of torment, Mr. James Ogston's wife and mistress each wanted Mr. James Ogston to leave the other but the Mister refused. It has been reported that the Macdonald Norwood Hall Hotel is haunted by the two lovers (Mister and Mistress) and the vengeful wife (Mrs.) who longs for revenge for the torrid years she had to endure from her husband. Love is not so patient or kind.

HISTORY

According to an article written by Haunted Rooms (2016), guests have reported active hauntings coming from the older section of the Macdonald Norwood Hall Hotel in Room1 (ghostly Mistress resides), Room 4 (ghostly Mr. James Ogston resides), Room 8 (our guest room), and Kitchen (ghostly Mrs. James Ogston).[1] These rooms are located at the top of a stairway. Pictures hanging in the dining room of the Mistress and Mister continually stare at each other while a light bulb positioned in a fixture to the right of the fireplace frequently burns out.

It is believed that James originally purchased Norwood in 1872 and rebuilt it in 1881 for his mistress so they could meet while he lived in Ardoe House across the river with his young family.[1]

Haunted Rooms (2016) also reveals that the apparition of James has been seen standing in front of the log fire in the dining room.[1] The ghost of his mistress has been reported to haunt the main staircase (perhaps looking for her lover). His wife is the most active of the three with reports of her being seen in the hallway, the kitchen, and the dining room.[1]

PRIOR HISTORY. In 1861, Mrs. Helen Morrison, wife of Baillie William Adamson (a London stockbroker) bought the property of Norwood. Mr. Adamson liked the name of Norwood and gave it to the house that he built on the land his wife had purchased.[2]

Mrs. Morrison then sold the property to John Taylor of Regent's Park just two years later. It was then later resold again in 1872 to a Colonel James (Soapy) Ogston, who partly rebuilt the house in 1881 before moving his family across the River Dee to Ardoe House and moving his mistress into Norwood.[2]

On the grounds of Norwood is where the ancient Pitfodels Castle once stood.[1] The foundations are likely still there but no remains of the house have been seen for the last fifty years.[2]

THE ENCOUNTER

On May 18, 2015, my husband and I stayed at the Macdonald Norwood Hall Hotel, Aberdeen, Scotland for one night. Upon our arrival, we made a request to be moved from the newer section of the hotel to the older section (known to be the most haunted). My husband and I stayed in Room 8 that was located near the top of the staircase. We were drawn to stay at the Macdonald Norwood Hotel after reading that it had an occasional haunting.

Art Illustration by Brandy Woods

252

Dead tired (no pun intended) upon arriving from our transatlantic airplane flight, we drove to this hotel, checked in, took a brief walk down the driveway admiring the property, and then, proceeded to go to supper at their in-house restaurant. Just after supper, we had a brief tour by a staff member of the public spaces within the hotel, learning of its history and of its resident ghosts. We went back to our room to settle in for the evening. It just so happens that I was too tired to set up my ghost equipment that evening and told my husband that I would have to simply "waive" my ghost hunting experience. I fell asleep quickly.

THE INCIDENT. Around 1:15 a.m.-1:30 a.m., my husband was awakened suddenly by "something" that sounded like a male voice calling out his name. He awoke in a panic (heart beating) looking around to see if someone was in our room. He saw no one. It was at the point when he heard his name called out that a loud THUMP or BANG sounded on the wall right next to him. Being curious, he went to the door, looked out into the hallway, saw no one on the stairs or in the area. Unusual for him, he remained terrified about that experience still talking about well into the next morning.

REPORTED NEXT MORNING. It was reported to us by staff that next morning that the Mistress' room and Mr. room were at the top of the stairs (Room 1 and Room 4).

We didn't know this at the time we were assigned to our room. We only knew that we were in the most haunted section of the hotel. It was also reported that the Mistress liked to frequent the stairs while the Mrs. liked to hang out in the kitchen. The Mr. and Mistress pictures hung in the dining room staring at each other. Their romance continued beyond death.

QUESTIONS AND THOUGHTS

Can owners who once lived at a property return in spirit even if they have been away from this home for a very long time? Yes. Places of comfort can attract the return of former residents. In this case, the Mister gave to the Mistress, the house as a gift. Why is the picture of Mrs. Ogston not hanging in the dining room next to the pictures of the Mistress and Mr. Ogston? Not clear. Who exactly called out my husband's name? Not clear. A male sounding voice.

Could my husband have been experiencing REM sleep when he heard his name and thump in the wall? No. How do I know this? In how he described the incident. When the THUMP occurred on the wall next to him, how does one not know that the sound was nothing more than a pipe clanking? My husband described hearing his name and the thump sound at the exact same time. Both together made this experience unusual and coincidental.

Tales of Apparitions #5

Chapter 22
Whistling – Old Firebug

Photo Illustration by Kelly Renee Schutz
Tales of Apparitions

Chapter 22
Whistling – Old Firebug

"Old Firebug. That was the name we called that old beater of a truck we use to drive around our neighborhood. My brother and I took turns driving it down the road tormenting our neighbors with it because it use to backfire into their yards as we opened it to full throttle. Of course, we had the greatest laugh about it. We were only allowed to take Old Firebug out for a spin during holidays and you know what happens on holidays – family gatherings in the backyards. We got the biggest kick out of hearing it POP POP ... POP POP POP as we passed Ms. Mallie's house. I swear, she had it out for us. She was probably the most likely to call the cops to put a stop to our screeching by her yard. Yep, those were the good old days. Old Firebug has since rested in peace behind the barn.

"I am sure Henry is appreciative that we didn't scrap the thing," I commented to my friend. "Who is Henry?" she asked. "Henry use to own this truck. He lived down the road about a mile and a half. He drove past our house every Saturday on his way to the local store to grab a bite and to play a round of cards with one of his buddies.

When he passed away unexpectedly, our father purchased Old Firebug from one of his family members who wanted to scrap it. The condition of it was a mess after his accident. But, my dad restored it right back to its original look. I think Henry is thankful for that.

"You know, if I didn't know better, I think Henry still hangs around that truck from time to time. On really still days, when I am behind the barn pulling weeds, I swear I can hear him whistling inside that cab. I would stop for a second, look up, and can just see him sitting there behind the wheel … happy, carefree, and on a mission to get his cup of coffee and play a round of cards with his buddies in town. I know he loved that old truck. Probably just my imagination, though. After all, why would he hang around?"

"How did Henry die?" my friend asked me. "Well, here is the story that was told to me," I commented.

"It was in the Fall of 1899. A nice day, full of sunshine during the morning and pouring rain in the afternoon. A light breeze kicked up some as a storm rolled in. The leaves were rustling in the breeze. Most fell to the ground after the storm rolled in and you could just see the reds, golds, and yellows all flitter to the ground.

"Henry needed to go to town to get a bag of feed for his hogs. While in town, he had his usual cup of coffee and played a round of cards with his buddies. When the storm rolled in, he decided he was going to try and get ahead of it, so he ventured back to his house in Old Firebug but decided to take a short cut. He decided to go down French Hill to save some time. French Hill was known for many accidents. The conditions of the road were dirt and when wet, became slippery. I guess Henry thought that Old Firebug was trustworthy enough to make it down that hill.

"As Henry approached French Hill, he put on his brake to try and grab the dirt better. The problem with doing that was he started to slip and slide and was being pulled into a deep ditch, located on the right side. He thought he was going to slide down the middle of the road but noticed another truck coming up the hill trying to gain speed. He had no choice but to avoid the truck and ended up in the ditch. Henry had broken his neck and died in Old Firebug. When they had his funeral, they parked his truck near the cemetery. It was all dented and mangled but it was what he would have wanted.

"I know this sounds like a really sad story but Henry loved that truck so much that he often commented that he would go to his grave in it. Well, I guess his wish came partially true. They couldn't bury him in it, some people do these days ... get buried in their vehicles or on their motorcycles ... but, back then, not even a thought.

"Let me show you his pride and joy. Now be real quiet as we go around the corner of the barn because if he is back there in the truck, I don't want to scare him away. *CREEPING behind the barn.*

"STOP ... LISTEN ... (whistling is heard coming from the inside of the truck) ... Do you hear that?" I said to my friend.
"No," she replies. "Listen harder," I said. It was at this point that a bird flew out of the broken truck window. "I would bet you heard a bird whistling, geezzz," she said.

"It wasn't him whistling, it was a bird," friend comments. "No, it was not a bird, it was Henry," I said. "Let's go ... maybe Henry will come around the corner and surprise us all -- BOO," friend mumbles.

As we walked away, all I could hear was a faint WHISTLING coming from inside the truck .... "Carry on, Henry ... Carry on, Old Firebug."

Chapter 23
Attacked in Haunted Museum

Composite by Kelly Renee Schutz
Illustrative

Chapter 23
Attacked in Haunted Museum

BACKGROUND

You have always wondered why you seem to attract paranormal energies to you. More importantly, you want to make sense of WHAT you have been attracting to put your situations into proper context.

The description of "energy" is a popular topic among paranormal researchers and investigators. "What is energy" ... "who is this energy" ... and ... "where do these energies come from?" Most importantly, "why and how do energies attach to objects giving the object power, affect, and motive in causing harm to others?"

As timing would have it, in the past several years, there have been an explosion of paranormal programs on television trying to answer these questions while educating us about "energy" and "unseen forces."

Many paranormal enthusiasts, like myself, have experienced varying levels of paranormal phenomena. We seek to educate ourselves with a course in "Paranormal Speculation 101" giving us a bit of insight into our experiences or vivid imaginations. Is that a ghost making your hair stand up on end or are you happy to see me? Ha-Ha-Ha.

One of the paranormal shows I found resonating with me early on was "Ghost Adventures." I liked how the show attempted to explain and debunk unexplained situations.

What I did not like about the show was when it began to grow in its popularity, it would attempt to educate us further by showcasing negatively charged haunted artifacts, some fatally dangerous, over the air waves. Yes, interesting ... but, dangerous and careless.

With the program's subtle disclaimer and warning to "look away" as the negative objects were shown ... it was obvious to me someone had no concern for the safety of its viewers OR lacked the insight in knowing HOW the showing of these negative artifacts would AFFECT its viewers. Seriously?

For whatever reason, I noticed these dangerous object episodes began diminishing and were not part of the regular series anymore. Good call, whatever the reason.

Zak Bagans would find a new platform to showcase his haunted objects. He would purchase an old mansion in Las Vegas, Nevada. He would turn this mansion into a haunted museum attraction.

This new platform would not only be a way of finding a home for his large collection of negatively charged artifacts but also a way to show the world that his haunted artifacts had power. 262

Case in point – he does not have to convince me anymore that his "building" and "artifacts" have power.

His main message – "negatively charged objects and environments can inflict harm." This brings us to the next question, "what do we do about it?"

THE PLATFORM

Zak Bagans is the lead investigator and personality of the popular television show "Ghost Adventures." As good timing would have it, he purchased an old mansion in Las Vegas, Nevada with the vision to reconstruct it into a haunted museum to house his large collection of negatively charged artifacts. His museum attraction would be filled with numerous artifacts from all over the world. Artifacts that have attached to them, "energies." Not just any energy – negative, hostile, and dangerous energies. This is no fun house experience.

Zak's museum continues to spike the interest of many [skeptics to believers] who travel from all parts of the world to experience and debunk his claims. He relays countless warnings about the dangers lurking about in the museum asking people to be mindful of their thoughts, emotions, and experiences.

If you want to tour this museum, you will sign a waiver releasing damages incurred to you while experiencing the visit. This is not a gesture of sensationalism.

MUSEUM IN CONSTRUCTION

Let us start from the beginning. In the summer of 2016, my husband and I planned a trip to Las Vegas. During our trip, we decided to drive to the location of the haunted museum to see how construction was moving along. Situated in a poor area of town with many homeless roaming about, a gate surrounded the museum guarded by security on all sides. Museum to open the Fall of 2017.

The mansion, constructed in 1938, is one of the oldest residencies in the area. The home was built for banker Cyril Wengert and his family. After the Wengert family sold the home, it housed employees working for the Nevada Bar Association. After the Nevada Bar Association moved out, the building-residence sat idle for a couple of years. Zak Bagan believed the location and building were ideal for his haunted artifact collection. Reconstruction begins.

It is my understanding Zak was not aware this home was demonically charged. Even when the Nevada Bar Association resided there, strange occurrences would frolic about inside the building. A satanic pentagram would be discovered in the basement. Unusual and unexplained energies would affect and follow home some of the most vulnerable workers.

Call this discovery "an added bonus" after the fact. What are the chances you are purchasing a building that is already demonically charged for your haunted exhibit?

THE VISIT IN 2016

Before my husband and I ventured to the museum, I made it a point to research anything I could find on others experiences near or inside the property. I wanted to gain an understanding of "what" others were perceiving.

Report 1. A report was found on a couple who drove around the museum late at night seeing a black shadowy figure meander across the lawn shape shifting itself into the form of a cat. My first thought, "under the influence?"

Report 2. Another report that several construction workers quit on site after having unexplained experiences scaring them. I recall reading a news article sharing this news and a concern the museum would not be finished by the Fall 2017 due date. There came a point where no construction worker wanted to go in or near the building. My initial thought was, "what is going on at this property that could be so bad?" In my own comparison, "after all, I survived a cycling mirror in Europe that scared the bejesus out of me. What could be any worse than that?"

THE MIST

During my husband's and my visit in the summer of 2016, we were able to park in a lot next to the museum. I wanted to take a few pictures. I got out of the car and walked over to the fence. We were at the museum at 2:00 PM. The weather was a perfect day, sunny, with the temperature its usual 90+ some degrees.

Photo 1 (arrows), what I am showing you is a large MIST surrounding the tree and steps. Compare to Photo 2. The mist is not a sprinkler. Not a laundry vent area. Not condensation steam. Not a glare from the fence or sun.

Did I see this mist when I was taking the picture? No. I wanted to snap my pictures and get out of there. I do recall seeing construction workers on the other side of the house and their making a lot of noise. I can only speculate the mist (apparitions) did not like the loud activity and decided to sit outside for a few minutes.

Photo 2. Comparison. This image was shot within 5 to 10 seconds after Photo 1. The delay was caused by my shoving my camera through the fence. Look at the tree and steps in the lower left corner. Clear as a bell. Same conditions.

MUSEUM IN 2019

Three years later, your sister wants to go to Las Vegas with you to tour the haunted museum. Knowing your energy attracts apparitions, even in daylight, you explain to her that you are hesitant about going inside that building for fear you will be "hunting season" for the ghosts. Especially since you already captured a MIST outside the building in plain daylight. How many people have done that? You agree to go with your sister to the museum.

FEBRUARY 2019

On a beautiful early morning in February, you and your sister arrive to Las Vegas. You feel tired from the plane trip. After a quick breakfast, you head to Zak Bagans Haunted Museum to get in line for your tickets. You arrive mid-morning around 11:00-11:30 AM.

Prior to arriving at the museum, you ask your sister to put on a cross-angel necklace you made for her and ask she tuck it under her shirt. You keep yours outside of your shirt as a symbol to the ghosts to leave you alone.

As you wait in line (as they only bring 10 people in at a time), you feel yourself getting edgy and anxious. Your sister is thrilled to be at the museum. You, not so much.

Flashbacks of reports you have heard about people visiting inside – (1) throwing up out on the lawn, (2) bloody noses, (3) scratched, (4) anxiety attacks, (5) fainting,

(6) cannot breathe, (7) heart attacks, (8) punches in stomach, (9) nightmares [followed home], (10) etc. The list goes on and on. You ask yourself, "why am I here?" Oh yes, ... material for my book.

You remind yourself that not everything is behind glass. The basement, where the satanic pentagram was discovered, is home to a rather nasty energy. You know your not going down into the basement but who is to say whatever is down there will not decide to take a mid-morning float around the museum?

To get tensions flowing, as part of the process, a man ("Jack") dressed in a topcoat and hat walks down the "wait line" handing out a form that needs to be signed. It is a waiver stating you understand the dangers of the museum and agree to not hold the owners liable.

As soon as you enter the building (ticket room) ... the haunted activity begins.

DEFINITIONS

Agent – a living person who is the focus of poltergeist activity. **Authentication** – proving genuine verification of facts surrounding an occurrence of paranormal phenomena. **Chance** – random, unpredictable influences on events. **Clairaudience** – auditory form of ESP paranormal info received outside range of normal perception through voices, whispers, auditory impressions.   269

Earthbound – a ghost or spirit that is unable to cross over at the time of death. **Ghost** – a ghost is believed to be the soul or the life force of a person or animal. **Ghost Hunter** – a person who attempts to gather information of paranormal activity. **Intelligent Haunting** – an interaction on the physical plane as in communication or object movement from a spirit who is conscious. **Manifestation** – the appearance or taking of form of an entity. **Materialization –** the formation of a visible physical form of a spirit. **Matrixing –** when the mind attempts to manifest images of something they are not.

Place-Centered Haunting – a location where paranormal events frequently take place. **Poltergeist** – non-human entity (noisy ghost) usually more malicious or destructive than ghosts or deceased human beings. May involve thumping, banging, levitation or movement of objects, stone throwing, and starting fires. **Skeptic** – to question what others may perceive as real or true. **Trance** – is a state of semi-consciousness in which a person is not self-aware and is either altogether unresponsive to external stimuli or selectively responsive following the directions of the person who has induced the trance. Trance states may occur involuntarily and unbidden. **Touched** – act of having physical contact from a spirit-entity such as pulling hair, shirt tugging, pushing, or tapping shoulders-backs.

BATHROOM PARANOIA

While I was getting tickets in the main lobby, my sister was trying to wrap her head around why she felt so paranoid while in the bathroom.   270

I said nothing about the feeling I had in the ticket room and told her I needed a few more pictures before the tour began. Low light. Creepy room. Nice scary beginning.

TICKET LOBBY. When they say, "let the fun begin" ... they are not kidding. While my sister was trying to calm herself down, I finished shooting a few pictures in the lobby.

I noticed my pictures were turning out blurry with white rods showing up. I shook my attempts off as low lighting conditions or specialized effects. Little did I realize, while I was trying to notice what was in the room, something was watching me from within the Shirley Temple exhibit. See circle below. Difficult to see. Not a reflection or face matrix. Nothing on shelf. Face of a man looking at me.

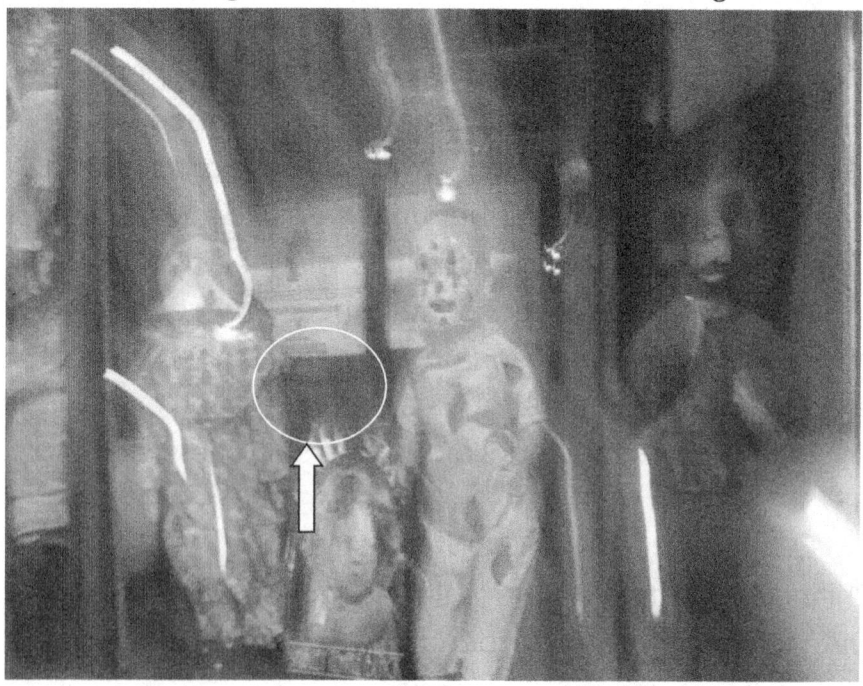

ODDITIE ENTRANCE. After we left the ticket lobby, we got in line to start the tour at one of the side doors. A tour guide begins the adventure by asking if anyone wanted to knock on the door. My sister was anxious to knock but I told her not to. Would you touch a haunted door?

ADVENTURE CONTINUES

In my moving from one room to the next, my overall feeling for nearly half the tour was that of peacefulness [no affect, clear minded, full energy, conscious]. In fact, I felt like I was walking through an antique store artifact gazing.

As the tour evolved, I found myself becoming so comfortable and non-threatened with the experience that I let my guard down. It was at THIS point I could feel the unseen forces acting up around me.

DOOR ROOM. The first room we entered from the outside had a mixture of dolls and unusual (odd) figures. Bizarre object collection room. If anything, the odd'ness of seeing "the unusual" began messing with my head.

LILLIE. I recall we were introduced to a doll by the name of Lillie. I believe she came from Germany. Her hair was from a deceased child. I cannot recall her story but she was cursed and had the energy to cause harm.

The tour guide introduced us to her. We spoke to her as if she was a real human being. We commented on how lovely her hair was. At the point of our response, the monitors in the room started acting up. My speculation at this point was that it was a visual trick to create nervousness. The phrase that always gets me is, "I've never seen this before." Recall I wrote about this in a previous chapter. Was this expression a lie? Will never know I suppose.   273

A side note. We were not allowed to take pictures inside the museum [only the ticket lobby]. Going through this experience, I will have to express … "good rule!"

Back to Lillie. If you were not nice to her [the doll], she would bring you bad luck. I know some of you would probably comment, "how would I know the difference in my life?"

DOLL ROOM. Adjacent to the odditie room was a room filled with a large collection of "haunted" dolls. Very few tourists were allowed to enter that room. I did not go in there. It was here we were introduced to what would be the "main" performers throughout the museum … little people (midgets).

Although I felt these actors were being exploited, as the museum was scary enough the way it was set up, I realize they were entitled to find work.

As we drifted from one room to the next looking at numerous artifacts, there came a point when the energy around ME began to change.

COFFIN ROOM. We entered a room set up like a church setting. I would say there were about 30 chairs set up. All facing 1-2 open coffins positioned at the front. These coffins contained the skeletons of "real" deceased people lying within them.

How Mr. Bagans was given permission to obtain and display two deceased skeletons remains sealed in paperwork.

As we walked into the room, I recall the storyteller (midget) standing in front yelling loudly (gruff) ... "can you tell me which chair a black shadow person rose up from underneath it"? Black shadow figures, by the way, are 99.5% demonic. Nothing to mess with and not a ghost.

As he asked this question, I felt my arm rise and my mouth mumble, "this one" (pointing to the chair my sister had just sat in). I was right. She jumps out of it.

As I sat there listening to the storyteller (midget with attitude), it was not long before I felt myself feeling sick. Nauseated. Dizzy.

Was something being pumped into that room to cause this feeling? Why was I suddenly feeling ill? Was this a psychological experiment?   I recall reading about many people feeling sick in the coffin room. They were right.

As I sat in my chair trying to relax with my sister two chairs away, seconds later, I now feel like something is lightly clawing at or scratching my back. Not an itch ... like scratch, scratch, scratch. Small scratches, not deep welts. I knew I was being marked.

I was in this room for its duration (regardless). Some people left after 30 seconds. At the point I started feeling ill, I began openly rubbing my cross-angel necklace. It was at this point where the assaults on my body would become noticeable. Something had its eye on me.

PUPPET ROOM. Speaking of feeling watched. Being the last out of the coffin room, I found myself becoming disoriented. A tour guide led me down to the puppet room where I squished myself in among the others.

As the next storyteller (midget) came out from a back room wearing a creepy mask, I found him to be mean and mouthy.

I also recalled in reading someone's story that you should never be the last person leaving the puppet room. Guess who left that last two rooms last? ME.

As I stood there along with the rest observing all the puppets (everywhere) on magnetic strings and sitting on shelves ... my eyes took note of one that appeared to be a witch. This one was in front of me hung by a string.

By the way, the purpose for the magnetic strings was to alert you if something paranormal was in the room. This electrical charge would activate the string and move the puppet. Interesting.

Picture yourself standing looking at a bunch of hanging puppets (around you and in front of you). You cannot help but notice a few. This witch puppet, to me, was particularly spooky.

As my eyes gazed at it, what I noticed was all the other puppets near her were not moving on their strings. However, she was moving. Was I causing this movement? As she was turning about, she stopped and was staring directly at me.

Being distracted and caught off guard, all I heard was mumble coming from the gruff storyteller (little person performer). He made some snide comment to me and I blew it off. I thought to myself, "great, now I am being harassed by a little person and targeted by a witch puppet."

I decided to take on the challenge and stare back at the witch puppet. Mistake.

I cannot recall why the storyteller was mouthing off to me ... I figured he was so possessed with negative energy that he did not realize what planet he was on. Personally, I wanted to slap him silly.

Well, I was the last one who left the room. Mistake. As we were guided down the hallway to the sideshow room, I felt a bit phased (dizzy, disoriented).

SIDESHOW ROOM. As we entered the sideshow room, I positioned myself to be the first one leading the pack out of there to the next destination. Standing amongst the crowd, we watched a young man(performer) stick a hook through his tongue while holding up a pail of rocks. If I recall this correctly, he also did an act using a power screwdriver. How does one clap when you are appalled by what you are seeing? And, as usual, the little person storyteller who would jump out from a back door only to accompany the sideshow performer with his act.

Although I felt a bit dazed going into this room ... I felt alright entering the sideshow room. There came a point when the sideshow performer said, "yes, I witnessed an apparition of an older man standing in that doorway, who manifested and disappeared before my eyes." "He was wearing a Victorian-styled dress coat/suit." I recalled seeing a video with a tourist being touched in this room.

However, it was at the point when we were leaving this room and walking up a back stairwell that would puzzle me for the rest of my life. We were on our way to a clown, mirror, and dybbuk box room.

As I was leading our group up a dark stairwell, I found myself, out of nowhere, drained. Energy drained. To the point of having none. Wanting to pass out. I struggled to get up to the top without passing out on the stairs. When I got to the top, I stumbled like a drunk person, waivered past our tour guide and grabbed a wall.

It was at this point I went into a full trance possession standing with my back against a wall. I recall my eyes closing. I could hear my sister yelling (panicked). I was not able to respond.

It was at this point I heard the tour guide call someone on her walkie talkie with a commotion about to gather around me. The tour guide, sideshow performer, little person, my sister, and probably video cameras all on me.

It felt like forever before I was able to open my eyes. Still feeling like I had no energy. What I saw in front of me were three to four shadows of people (no features).

The tour guide had tried to talk to me. I recall mumbling to her that I was an empath. She asked me if I was able to continue with the tour or be ushered down a back door. I asked her what lied ahead (clown room). I told her I wanted to finish the tour. **What I realized by the end of the tour was that my "rubbing" my cross openly provoked the negative spirits to challenge me back.**

CLOWN ROOM. My sister was my hero that day. Approaching the "clown room" (75 life sized clowns), with the usual fog effects ... I could only imagine what lied ahead. From the way I felt, if anyone dared jump out at me, I would have given it a three-pound punch.

My sister led me through the clown maze (loud music, lots of fog, loud clown laughing). Good god. Let me say – I am not afraid of clowns ... just am not fond of them.

At the point of leaving the clown room, I felt whatever was inside of me was finally LEAVING. I could feel it lifting out of me. As it was leaving my body, my energy began to return.

Who was it? What was it? Where did it come from? Questions I will never figure out. A very real experience.

DYBBUK BOX ROOM. From the clown room, this led us into the mirror, cry boy painting, AND of course, the famous dybbuk box room. I declined going into the dybbuk box room. I asked my sister to not spend a lot of time in there. People have been known to pass out, have heart attacks, and odd health issues in that room.

After all, I speculate it knew I was on my way. Yes, I believe the dybbuk box had a hold on me. I have watched on documentaries (television) how it had put people in trances before. I was no different.

Even though the dybbuk box was behind glass, reports from others experienced its glass surround vibrating without touching it. Videos have also shown people having ambulance rides from that room.

What makes that box so powerful? Look up its story on the Internet. Yes, this box has an ability to affect and kill you.

PEGGY ROOM. I decided to go into the Peggy Room. As we crammed ourselves into a tight space, the tour guide shut the door behind us. Peggy, a life-sized doll, is cursed.

The last thing you want to do is mock it, say something disrespectful, or challenge it. Peggy, like Robert the Doll, has strong, remarkable abilities to cause harm.

So, here we are. Standing there in front of Peggy the Doll. She stood behind a glass case. We were told not to bring up Lillie as she is jealous of this doll getting attention.

We asked Peggy questions. Next to it was a white noise device that would say words if she responded. We stood there complimenting it. After all, who wants to be attacked? The doll is known to give people nose bleeds.

However, it was near the point of leaving when I said to the tour guide, "although Peggy's voice sounds female, is that really a male in disguise?" She told me, "yes."

How did I know Peggy wasn't a "she" but rather, a "he." Hiding in a female doll. Peggy, in my view, is a demon … which really makes her-he an IT.

Peggy will only allow specific people to touch or hold her causing no harm. Looking into her eyes is a risk only few tour guides take.

CHARLES MANSON ROOM. How Mr. Bagans managed to get his hands on some of Charles Manson's cremation ashes is beyond me. He must have contacted his grandson and paid him for some.

Someone drew a pencil sketch of Charles Manson's face and used his cremation ashes for the eyeball area. The sketch is behind glass, as everything is.

Zak shares on Twitter a video of a young gal (tourist) who mocked Mr. Manson while looking at this sketch finding herself being attacked with the feeling of being stabbed in the belly numerous times.

In my opinion, it is 50-50 coin toss that this attack came directly from Mr. Manson. After all, that building is riddled with negative forces having the liberty to float around.

What was perhaps the most shocking to me was the vast collection of artifacts like false teeth, objects, and of course, images from beloved Hollywood personalities, who apparently, had a dark side to them.

In a private room, the visual-audio story of a woman who became possessed by a demon she could not rid ...

documenting herself as she was dying.

DEATH STAIRS. When I lived in Indiana, it was well known that a home that resided in Gary, Indiana was demonically possessed. The story of this house and tortured family had been featured on television many times. Mr. Bagans purchased the home for investigation.

I taught college students. It was when one of my students told me he intended to break into that house to "find ghosts" that worried me. It just so happens with all the national news about it and break ins ... Mr. Bagans had to tear the house down. What Mr. Bagans kept from that house was the stairway that went down into the basement (believed to be haunted with a demonic presence). He placed that stairwell behind glass in his museum.

When I was in that room, I felt nothing. As in all his rooms, we would cluster together as a group and the tour guides would shut the doors behind us. Adds to the fear factor.

OTHER ROOMS. Every room told several stories. This museum is large and full of negatively charged artifacts. It was at the point when we left the Natalie Wood's room where I was standing next to a door that Mr. Bagans suddenly came out of nearly hitting me with it.

Mr. Bagans made his appearances like this to give his visitors a chance (glance) to see him.

GIFT SHOP. After the final room, we were funneled through their gift shop. It was in this room that my sister was chatting with Mr. Bagan's mother.

Something told me she was awaiting our arrival [after my being attacked]. She came across as a nice woman but rather guarded.

When someone is attacked in their building, regardless of signed paperwork ... of course, this will raise eyebrows. My attack may have evolved from scratching to being watched by a puppet to a full-blown trance possession ... but my experiences in there were not taken lightly.

Tourists have experiences in that museum every day. From the mild to severe. Even though they say they are not held liable ... I use to work in law ... everyone can be sued, regardless of signing a piece of paper.

Is that museum haunted? Yes. Does it have at least one negative force? Yes. Demonic? Yes. Unexplained ... yes. Would I ever want to go back in there again? I would need to wear a space suit with nail spikes.

FOLLOWS ME TO MY HOTEL ROOM. When my sister and I were about to leave the museum, we sat in the car for a few minutes while I collected myself. I still felt a bit off.

We watched a couple "saging" each other in the parking lot. I pointed out to my sister that this is what we should be doing as I did not want anything attached or following us back to our room.

As we sat there, we decided to get out of the car and chat with the security guard who was positioned at the exit door. He told us that Mr. Bagan's mother hated going into the museum alone at night [do not blame her in the least].

He said they would get numerous security breach "warnings" that something had broken into the museum. Only to find out when searched, nothing had been there. The ghosts are setting off the security alarms.

When my sister and I returned to our hotel room, I told her I still felt a bit off. She left the room momentarily. I read a religious prayer out loud to rid any attachments. As I went to the restroom, I noticed the shower curtain flinging up as if something were hiding behind it leaving in a hurry. This moment did not phase or scare me. I told my sister when she returned to the room that whatever was in the bathroom is now gone. The expression on her face [stunned] said it all.

WINNING JACKPOTS. Maybe being in a trance is not so bad if you want to win money. It was obviously my lucky night. That evening I won several jackpots on a few machines. I just kept winning and winning.

A rough airplane ride home causing me to go into shear panic would bring us back to Minnesota. I cannot stand rough turbulence or delayed arrivals.

We stayed overnight in a casino due to weather issues. The next morning, I recall seeing a FLASH of a buffalo enter my mind as I woke up. I went down to play a buffalo slot machine and won $3200.00.

That was a profitable trip. Of course, the IRS got their share.

Coincidences? Read Chapter 10 (Book 10, Message Received) on my winning jackpots. Since 2017, I have won 18 jackpots. Big ones – small ones. I have noticed my brain frequency changes when I am in casinos.

FINAL THOUGHTS – WORDS TO LIVE BY
My trip to Zak Bagans Haunted Museum validates to me that negative unseen forces (energies) do exist. It also validates when I am dreadfully tired or in a trance-like mindset ... I seem to affect and/or trigger electronics. If I am not triggering electronics ... then, my mind seems to know where to find a winning slot machine.

Most importantly, my rubbing my cross-angel necklace provoked the negative ghosts in that museum. Their message back to me was, "do you really think that cross is going to protect you?" The answer is, "no."

Illustration by Brandy Woods

THE HOTEL ROOM

After we arrived at our hotel from leaving the Zak Bagans Haunted Museum experience, I laid down in bed placing a bible on my chest to remove any negative attachments.

I was determined to rid whatever followed me from there off me so I could get my normal "self" back in motion. Did it work? Whatever was in the bathroom left in a hurry.

Chapter 24
Lady Catherine

Illustration–Photo Taken by Kelly Renee Schutz
True Story

Dalhousie Castle Hotel, Edinburgh, Scotland

Chapter 24
Lady Catherine

COINCIDENTAL RESEMBLANCE

In an article updated on October 22, 2013 in an online newspaper called The Daily Record (**www.dailyrecord.co.uk**) as circulated in the United Kingdom, the author who wrote *Lovelorn Lady Catherine Haunts Dalhousie Castle* questions if it is Lady Catherine, a troubled 16-year old teenager, who continues to haunt the 800-year-old Dalhousie Castle in Midlothian. Midlothian resides near Bonnyrigg, Edinburgh, Scotland.

It was assumed Lady Catherine died of a broken heart after being banished to the castle tower in 1695 after being caught with a stable hand. She starved herself to death.

The alleged Lady Catherine appears at weddings in the form of a noticeable white mist (when photographed). What is even more daunting is this young girl dressed in a white gown is not only standing next to a staircase with a mist present around her BUT, the little unknown girl strikes a very odd resemblance to a picture that was hanging in my room, Room 1, when we were there late May 2015. See images on the next three pages. In my attempt to find out the identity of the picture hanging in Room 1, no one responded.

SIDE NOTE: Not all artwork hanging in castles are original to their homes. Some artwork is purchased at garage sales. Castle piper Andrew Sharp, on occasion, feels he sees Lady Catherine stalking the corridors, turrets, and dungeon.

According to the article, many people who have seen Lady Catherine have thought she was staff with her grey dress with the puff sleeves, sharp features and tiny feet in little pointed shoes. Only when she disappears through locked doors do guests get a fright. Others have reported seeing a woman in their rooms, waving from windows or merely sitting at the end of their beds. Woman or teenager?

King Edward I, or Longshanks, stayed at the castle on his way to meet Sir William Wallace at the Battle of Falkirk and Oliver Cromwell used the castle as a base for his invasion of Scotland. It was converted in 1972 into a hotel.

SCREEN SHOT
YOUTUBE VIDEO OF HAUNTING

On the previous page, a YouTube video uploaded on August 22, 2009 showing documentation of a ghostly encounter that occurred in the castle's dungeon when Helen Parker, a news reporter for new.com.au, attempted to investigate the castle in search of a haunting. YouTube video, "Dalhousie Haunted Castle Ghost Story - Dalhousie Castle, Bonnyrigg, Edinburgh, Scotland." The link is: **https://www.youtube.com/watch?v=Aq74DXr2aAU**

GHOSTLY CHILD RESEMBLANCE

Photo of Image Taken by Kelly Renee Schutz
Lady Catherine? Identity Unknown, Portrait in Room

MIST

Compare
Child's Face

MIST

Identity of Child Unknown
White Mist Near Child Who Resembles Portrait

Chapter 25
Haunted Jerome Grand Hotel

1917 (Old Hospital); Reconstructed 1926; Closed 1950

UNITED VERDE HOSPITAL CIRCA 1939

Chapter 25
Haunted Jerome Grand Hotel

PHENOMENA

The Jerome Grand Hotel, located in Jerome, Arizona is presumed to be haunted by several ghosts. What use to be a hospital constructed in 1917, reconstructed in 1926, closed around 1950. It was maintained while abandoned for 44 years, watched by local police (1980's) before new owners purchased it around May 1994. The hotel was renovated by new owners with new paint, carpet, beds, etc. causing some apparitions to act up about the changes. According to various sources, approximately 9000 people (sickness, pain, death) died in the United Verde Hospital during its operation. No known records exist to verify or explain this number as to causes.

JEROME GRAND HOTEL
As of March 25, 2022

Permission to Copy from Website

The United Verde Hospital was constructed in 1926, to replace the old hospital constructed in 1917, when a fault shift, due to blasting, damaged the south wing.

Once patients and equipment were moved to the new hospital in January 1927, the wing was removed. With some major remodeling, the Clubhouse building that stands today, is missing the south wing. Another building, the original Jerome High School, was damaged by the same fault and had to be torn down. An additional major building, the United Verde Apartments, was missed by one foot from being damaged by the same fault.

The strange location for the 4th and last hospital built (now the Jerome Grand Hotel) was due to the known stability of the ground. The building plans date back to February 1926, and this 30,000 sq. ft. poured in place concrete building was opened in January 1927. It featured patient call lights, balconies, sun porches, emergency backup lighting, Otis self-service elevator, ice making room in Arizona, laboratories, X-ray, major and minor surgical facilities, men's, women's, and children's wards, private and semi-private rooms, blanket warming closets, and housing for some staff.

In 1930, the hospital was considered the most modern in Arizona and possibly the Western States. William Clark used the hospital as a marketing tool to attract the best employees. Good housing, great schools, and the top medical care available.

The building was originally equipped with three boilers. The 50 Horsepower Kewanee low pressure steam boiler for heat is still being used. A high-pressure steam boiler for sterilization, which was given away to be used on a steam engine and a hot water boiler, which was next to the now red 1000 gal. hot water tank, had to be replaced due to missing parts. The boilers are all placed in a pit designed to both serve as a place to flush out the boilers and catch water from two weep drains from the building foundation. Water released into the pit flows to a lower tank from which it is pumped out. The vacuum or recovery tank collects condensed steam (water) from the radiators and then pumps it back into the steam boiler.

The system remains fully automated as it was originally designed. The Kewanee Boiler Company and Nash Engineering Company (manufactured vacuum systems) were in business in the 1990's and provided information and some parts. The over 90-year-old GE motors still work the vacuum pumps.

Phelps Dodge Mining Corporation acquired the United Verde Jerome Mine holdings in 1935 and continued to operate the United Verde Hospital until its closing in 1950. The hospital was maintained fully furnished for approximately 20 years, after which, Phelps Dodge knew it would never be used as a hospital in the future.

Most of the furnishings were removed in the 1970's and 1980's. Phelps Dodge would hire a live-in caretaker or lease it to a family just to keep it occupied and safe from vandals.

DEATH OF CARETAKER

Manoah was found hanging from a steam pipe in the Engineer's Office, where he resided as a caretaker. After his death in 1982, the building was boarded up and watched over by the local police and small staff still at the Phelps Dodge Headquarters in Jerome. While some vandalism did occur, this added an incentive, for liability reasons, for Phelps Dodge to sell the property.

In December 1993, an offer to purchase was made to the Phelps Dodge Corporation by Larry and Sarah Altherr, of Phoenix, Arizona. Possession was taken on May 29, 1994. Larry and Sarah Altherr still own and operate the Jerome Grand Hotel (as of March 25, 2022).

ROYALS ROYCE

In 2003, an added fixture to the building was, and still is, parked in the hotel garage. The 1928 Springfield Rolls-Royce Phantom I Lonsdale has been driven to Phoenix, Flagstaff, Prescott and Sedona and is used for parades or shows. The car is in original condition for the most part and sports a Brewster body.

The car has just under 93,000 miles and was made in America. Rolls-Royce produced cars in Springfield, Massachusetts for 10 years saving import fees on their cars from England and providing the U.S. with the steering wheel on the correct side. Some features used on the American built cars first were then used on the English models such as bumpers and a chassis lubricating system.

HOTEL and TOWN SHOPS

Driving up to the Jerome Grand Hotel is a bit of a challenge. Driving through the town's winding, pig tail-like streets, you leave Hwy 89A, enter Hill St. (right) which starts out as a one lane, turning into a two-way road up to the hotel. There is parking in front of the building and down the hill.

The Palace Restaurant, now Haunted Hamburger, was opened in 1994 and is located across from Hill Street. This was the first restaurant serving lunch and dinner to have dependable hours and was the first to start attracting people one level above downtown.

Few people drove in 1926 when the hospital was built and only twelve parking spaces were provided. Over 1000 dump truck loads were excavated to make the now 70 spaces around the Hotel and Restaurant. Excavation was done during the first two years of renovation. It wasn't until July 1996, the first rooms were ready, and building opened.

In 1997, the Grand View Restaurant and Lounge were opened but it soon became apparent that leasing the Restaurant was a better plan and in 2003, the Asylum Restaurant was opened and continues. The renter of the Asylum chose its name which has no direct connection to what that part of the Jerome Grand Hotel was used for in the past.. The Asylum Restaurant building use to be the WAITING and INTAKE area to the United Verde Hospital.

MORE HISTORY

According to sources found on the Internet, the city of Jerome has burned to the ground nearly 4-5 times. Fire is a major concern for any hotel, new or old. The United Verde Copper Company insisted the hospital be built fire-proof and be able to withstand major blasting from the mines.

BE MINDFUL OF STORIES

My husband and I went on a tour in Sedona the day after our stay at the Jerome Grand Hotel. Just as our guide was about to end the tour, he decided to provide information about the history of Jerome and the Asylum Restaurant.

As we listened to him, we knew what he was saying was false information (not intentional, poorly informed). Most people believe tour guides give factual history. Most try to give the "facts", but some fail their test in history learning. Fact checking stories given by tour guides can be exhausting. Although his words about the Asylum Restaurant added interest, nothing he said was accurate. Even more embarrassing was when I corrected him in front of our group about his lack of fact checking.

The tour guide also stated was back in 1917-1927, approximately 15000 people who lived in or near Jerome died from influenza, Scarlett fever, or other diseases.

It is true that the population was near 15000. However, that number is not correct regarding "how many" passed away living in or near the town. Why is this important? Read below.

Sources indicate World War II greatly increased the demand for copper attracting several to the area. Once the war was over, the demand plummeted, and people left the town. The Phelps Dodge Mine closed in 1953. The remaining population of 50 to 100 residents promoted the town as a historic ghost town.

Going back to 1917-1927 ... speculation that 15000 people died from a pandemic outbreak was only a partial truth. Sources indicated there was a pandemic outbreak around 1918 with many people dying. However, the number remains unknown. I did see images of residents in the town of Jerome in 1918 wearing masks (on Internet).

The tour guide stated there were so many dead bodies that the funeral director didn't know what to do with them. Apparently, one solution was to cremate the deceased and use their ashes in the making of concrete blocks and paving materials used in the town of Jerome (streets, walkways, other). Supposedly, the pavement we drove on in and around Jerome (to this day) is/are of those deceased resident's ashes. A local historical society would need to fact check this story.

Many people believe Jerome is one of the most haunted towns in America. Personally, I disagree. The entire world is haunted. If it is true, that the cement we walked on was mixed with human ashes from the past ... this would be creepy. However, it doesn't mean their human souls remained in those ashes haunting the town with "sidewalks" or "pavement areas" as graves.

IS THE JEROME GRAND HOTEL HAUNTED?

Yes. Being a sensitive, empath, I can affirm there was something unusual about a few of the areas my husband and I explored in the hotel.

The owner stated there had been a couple of TV shows on the "spirit" nature of the Jerome Grand Hotel and several psychics visiting the property. The owner adds out of the many visiting psychics over the years, three of them seemed to pick up on both past and present. Two in particular, "the Head Nurse" / "the Nurse in charge" was upset with the removal of the dispensary desks.

Both psychics felt their visitations while in what is now the Restaurant/Lounge area (Asylum) and originally the dispensary and/or main entrance to the United Verde Hospital (waiting or intake room). The owner told each psychic the original dispensary desks were in storage. The psychics did not know each other visiting more than a year apart.

Later, upon leasing out he Restaurant/Lounge in 2003, the new tenant somehow saw two cabinets stored at the back of one of the garages in the hotel. He asked the owner what they were and if he could use them in the restaurant area. With permission granted, the original dispensary counter height desks were relocated within a few feet of their original placement. To date, according to the owner, the "Head Nurse" has made no more complaints – at least about the desks.

AUTHOR RESEARCH ON HAUNTS

Reports about the types of hauntings experienced in the building have varied.

A reviewer on Trip Advisor stated her wall clock, like the one pictured on page 304, had its front door opened while she was away at dinner. In my trying to open this door, it would be possible for an apparition to open the front door but with strong energy.

Another, investigator, felt sick and was unable to breathe while walking down the hallway on the 3rd floor. A couple reported their wardrobe cabinet door was opened in the morning after awakening.

A man reported being tripped off balance by something he could not see (animal under feet) as he was heading to the bathroom. Along this same line, several reported seeing a black cat in the hallway or in their bathrooms running away and disappearing.

Some even reported flying orbs, a translucent apparition wearing a wedding dress, and shadow figure at the end of a long hallway. Let's not forget about the many ghost hunters that come to explore the property conjuring up the unseen in their rooms.

STORY ON INTERNET

Written By and Credited to Kayla Rutledge & Connor Whitt
October 20, 2017

What is now the remnants of a once booming and innovative copper-mining city, Jerome is one of the most paranormal destinations in Arizona. One should not be fooled by the town's spooky appeal. Sitting on the side of a mountain, the town can offer ghost stories, Western character, and more.

At its peak, Jerome was home to 15,000 people, but today has approximately 400 residents. Despite the low population, the town has become a hotspot for tourism and people who seek out a thrilling adventure.

Kenneth Cooper, a Jerome resident and owner of **Ghost Town Tours**, thinks the town has a unique commitment to history. He noted it is important to preserve the pieces of Jerome that make it so unique, like its history of copper mining.

After hitchhiking his way to Jerome in 1998, Cooper fell in love with the small town, but he never expected how eerie Jerome would be. Cooper has said he's experienced the presence of the ghosts Jerome is reportedly known for and is not afraid for his safety when experiencing paranormal activity.

"One of my awakenings that helped me realize weird stuff happens here, was at the park late at night with just a couple friends. On a still summer night, all of a sudden, the swing set started moving by itself with no wind", said Cooper.

"A ghost is nothing more than a piece of the past that's still present. [Ghosts] work in mysterious ways. They keep those that respect them safe and look out for us."

Aside from finding enjoyment in the ghostly character of the town, Cooper has an incredibly strong appreciation for how close the community is. "[Residents of Jerome] are sacrificing a lot to be here," Cooper said. "[Ghosts] act in their own best interest, and they want the best neighbors."

Charlie DeBrito, a tourist from Florida, traveled to Jerome. On his first day in Jerome, with his camera around his neck, DeBrito was prepared for whatever he may see.

"I'm most excited for the scenery and the history. It used to be a boom town here, and now it's just not a boom town. But I came back because of its history," said Debrito. At the peak of one of the mountains in town, one building stands alone — the Jerome Grand Hotel. The massive yellow structure with maroon curtains was once a hospital transformed into a hotel in 1994.

Before the building attained its current hotel status, it was where many copper miners were treated.

Many miners, however, died in the process of working in the pits, and others died in the confines of what is now the Jerome Grand Hotel.

Emilee Due, front desk manager at the hotel (back in 2017), said miner's souls were lost on the way to the afterlife, and they now roam the halls of the hotel.

"[The building] opened in 1927 as the only hospital in the Verde Valley," said Due. "[Guests today] will hear noises in the hallways or get pictures of orbs on their cameras. Things might move around, or people might feel things or hear things." Hotel bartender Charlie Garrett has been working at the hotel for seven years, but he has not yet come across the presence of ghosts.

"Roughly 10,000 people have died in this building (United Verde Hospital), but thankfully I haven't come across any of their spirits yet," said Garrett.

Predominantly a copper-mining town in the past, reported incidents of paranormal activity have involved copper miners. Working in the pits, men were known to be some of the toughest people in the West. Conditions were rough, and each day working in the mines could be their last.

In the past, while men commonly worked mining copper, some women made a living in a different way. Prostitution was ubiquitous in the past, and a license was all that was required for a woman to work in prostitution.

The industry was profitable, but for **Marie Juanita, aka Sammie Dean**, profit came at a high price. Found dead in her room July 7, 1931, the cause of Juanita's death was deemed to murder by strangulations. Juanita's murder remains unsolved, and police gave up the search for her

killer. Juanita, however, has not given up her search. Her soul has been reported to linger around the town in search of resolution to her unsolved murder.

"It is my belief, living here, that you are put on this planet for a reason. And, if you are taken off this planet before your reason for being here has been fulfilled, the likelihood of you hanging around is going to be pretty great," said Jay Kinsella, former Mayor of the town and general manager of the Jerome Historical Society.

When Kinsella was mayor, he lived in the house where Juanita was found murdered. He experienced several paranormal occurrences in the home. Kinsella's children saw ghostly figures around the house. Top hat figure was a tall man dressed in a well-fitting suit and top hat, whom, is believed to be the ghost of Juanita's killer. Notably, the room she was murdered in is a hub for paranormal activity.

"You can tell the presence. When you go into that room, and you're the only soul in that room, you are not the only soul in that room," Kinsella said.

Though Jerome may be a small town tucked away by a mountainside, the history and reported presence of ghosts helps bring continued appreciation to the town. Residents of Jerome have a true passion for bringing people close to the antiquity the town has to offer.

INTERVIEWS - STAFF ENCOUNTERS

Thank you, Sarah, owner, who allowed me to interview and publish information in this book provided by Sheila and Bob, lobby desk managers, about their "experiences" and "haunts" in the hotel. Thank you, Sheila and Bob, for your time and information. I hope I have been able to write your stories in this book correctly.

SHEILA'S ENCOUNTERS

I met Sheila, afternoon-evening managerial staff, tending to the front desk on our (husband and I) way out to a UFO watching activity. A brief stop, I found Sheila to be a smart, observant, pretty gal who was open to discussions about paranormal activity. Sheila has been employed by the hotel for several years. She has encountered numerous sightings and sensations.

ENCOUNTER #1 - Although my husband and I were in a hurry to leave for the UFO watching activity, Sheila acknowledged (as did I) that she felt a small group (presence) of apparitions gathering around us listening in to my inquiry to her about the death of a maintenance guy found dead within the first-floor elevator. When my husband and I left Sheila, as we headed out the door, I felt incredible tingling throughout my entire body (a sign that I have one or more apparitions near or attached to me).

<u>SHEILA'S INTERVIEW</u>

Upon our return from the UFO watching activity, with paper and pen in hand, Sheila and I sat down to begin our interview. Sheila has abilities to hear (clairaudient), see (clairvisual), smell (clairsentient), and feel (clairsentient) ghostly activity. She is also a sensitive empath with some clairvoyant (able to sense future) abilities. Her abilities activate (like mine) when we are experiencing certain types of emotional moods.

It is believed the 3rd floor, where my husband and I were staying (Room 30), was designated (back in the day) for surgeries, treatment of severe injuries, delivery of babies, ICU, and nursery. A lot of energy was expended on that floor due to various emergencies. It was also noted the lead doctor (surgeon) resided or was his office) in the Grand Suite, which was at one time, attached to Room 30.

INCIDENT #1 – on Sheila's first night on the job (years ago) (3:00 AM), she saw a cowboy (apparition) standing near the grandfather clock in the main lobby. He was dressed to go out on the town. She noticed him. He spoke to her telepathically and disappeared. Not seen since.

INCIDENT #2 – during an evening shift, she and her manager were at the front desk. Sheila noticed a girl (apparition) (age 16-17) coming down the stairs that led into the lobby. The girl wore a green hospital gown, had wet, black shoulder length hair, and was very jittery. The apparition (gal) stood at the front desk for 15 minutes (jittery) looking at Sheila. The girl didn't speak. At no point in time did the manager see this jittery girl standing there. The gal faded away. Thirty days later, a staff member described seeing a girl with this description in her dreams. The staff member and Sheila had no conversation about her until she mentioned this dream.

INCIDENT #3 – Sheila would start having unusual dreams. Negative, dramatic, communicating apparitions, three men at a poker table, etc. Communication or attachment.

INCIDENT #4 – Nurse shows to Sheila saying, "I want to help." Shows in lobby around 2:00 AM. Along that same line, if Sheila accidentally swears, a nurse scolds her.

INCIDENT #5 – Young boy telepathically says to her, "hospital?" Making an inquiry or telling Sheila where he is.

INCIDENT #6 – Black cat (apparition) is sitting on the floor in the lobby and disappears in front of Sheila.

INCIDENT #7 – Sheila sees tall shadow figures in various locations of the hotel.

INCIDENT #8 – Sees surgeon as full apparition standing in the Grand Suite. Annoyed of her presence. Hands on hips. Black hair, white coat. She leaves immediately.

INCIDENT #9 – Three Hispanic ladies come into the front door of lobby and one says to Sheila that a woman with brown curly hair was standing right behind her. This woman was known as Gurtie May Patch. Gurtie was a patient in the psych ward (Room 37B). No one knows how she fell to her death out her window down to street level. Speculation, boyfriend pushed her out of window.

INCIDENT #10 – Sheila would smell occasional cigar smoke.

INCIDENT #11 – Sheila would have two situations experiencing high anxiety where she would have to go home. Along that same line, my husband experienced high anxiety on the 3rd floor while in the hallway but he couldn't figure out why it came on suddenly.

INCIDENT #12 – Sheila was aware the most haunted rooms would experience: (1) toilets flushing, (2) faucets turning on, (3) closet doors opening (Room 39B) and seeing a pendulum bounce against the glass tapping it continuously rather than moving from its typical side-side.

INCIDENT #13 – Sheila witnessed a tall shadow figure (wanderer) on the 4th floor going from Room 40-41-42-40. She telepathically tells this shadow figure It didn't have to confine itself to this area. A staff member sees this shadow figure in the laundry room a few days later.

INCIDENT #14 – Sheila's scariest haunt was in the boiler room seeing an apparition duck behind an object.

INCIDENT #15 – Sheila comes to work through the front lobby doors. As soon as she opens the doors, she hears a nursery rhyme sing in her head. Came out of nowhere.

SHEILA LOOKS LIKE FORMER NURSE

They say, we all have a double of ourselves running around. However, how do we explain our being drawn to a haunted hotel (for work) where a former nurse looks identical to us in all features? Sheila looks <u>identical</u> to this former nurse (no known relationship). The nurse was at this hospital for one year (1945-1946) before moving to Ohio. Coincidence? I don't think so.

Ruth Fields Johnson local Jerome girl, started her nursing career as a nurses aide in the United Verde Hospital (1945-46)

BOB'S INTERVIEW

Thank you, Bob, for adding in your two cents. Bob is a handsome gentleman who would not consider himself to be sensitive. He has worked for the Jerome Grand Hotel for nearly 15 years. He would consider himself to be a skeptic-believer (indifferent). Bob tells me he has always tried to debunk unusual happenings, or he simply ignores them. However, at the Jerome Grand Hotel, nothing is ignored.

INCIDENTS

- Is stationed at the lobby desk (evening). Switchboard rings, no one there. Unusual.
- Front doors to building opens on own. No wind. No explanation. Too heavy to open on own.
- Elevator is activated, comes down to lobby, no one steps out of it or is in it. Must activate by a key.
- Hears a clear voice that says, "excuse me." Looks up and no one is there.
- Other situations – tries to not focus heavily on unexplained situations but wonders about them.

CLAUD HARVEY

In 1935, Claud Harvey, was a maintenance worker for the hospital. He stayed in Room 12. He was an apprentice. He had an argument with someone that led to his death. He was found face down, arms by his sides, head pinned, by or near (inside) elevator, first floor. Obvious he was beat up in a fight. Reason? Unknown. No autopsy was performed. Not sure if they ever convicted or found murderer. Why is this interesting? Look below.

This picture was taken a few months before Claud's death. Claud is located on the 2nd level, far right, person with no face (darkened out).

When Claud saw this picture, as all, puzzled as to why his face didn't show. He made a joke about it. A few months later, he is dead.

I am a professional photographer. The only way an image shows black is if it is exposed to light at processing. Not the case here. The men in front of him are a little dark but not due to processing.   316

Was something or someone providing a warning to Claud? Who killed Claud Harvey?

OUR ENCOUNTERS

Did my husband and I have any encounters? Yes. Were these situations imagined? No.

My husband and I stayed at the Jerome Grand Hotel on March 23, 2022 for one night. We stayed in Room 30 (3rd floor). This room (back in the day) was a baby nursery (newborns and mothers).

The entire 3rd floor was designated for delivery of babies, their mothers, operations, and ICU. A lot of energy was expended throughout this floor causing heightened anxiousness and excitedness everywhere (imprint).

I had asked Sarah (owner) if there were any reports of hauntings in our room. She stated guests reported smelling baby powder in Room 30 and sometimes heard babies cry. Yes, we smelled the baby powder but passed this smell off as cleaning products. No, we did not hear babies cry. Yes, as we walked down the 3rd floor hallway, my husband felt incredibly anxious (but couldn't figure out why). No, we didn't see orbs. My K2 meter rarely blinked.

My experiences occurred by the check-in desk near the elevator where the maintenance man, Claud was murdered.

CHECK-IN

Upon check-in, I inquired with Sarah (owner) if I could receive her permission to interview a few of her staff about their paranormal experiences at the hotel. Granted.

As my husband and I proceeded to the Otis elevator to go our room, as the elevator doors opened, I felt a presence near me (full body tingling). I felt this presence ride the elevator with us. My husband felt nothing.

We proceeded to Room 30 where I smelled the baby powder scent in the room upon entering. One needs to be reminded about "self-sabotaging" thoughts. Tell someone there is a powder smell and you automatically smell it.

I called down to the front desk on the antique phone located on my dresser in our room to ask about dinner options. The static heard on the other end could be misinterpreted as paranormal. However, because I use to own a few operational antique phones, the static sound to me, was nothing more than a wiring issue.

Sarah had mentioned that the television in our room had a connection issue that was being worked on. This is important to note as most ghost hunting enthusiasts would try and pass something like this off as paranormal.

Neither of us felt or seen anything as we walked to dinner (Asylum Restaurant). However, when we left to go UFO watching, I met Sheila (evening desk staff), at the front desk. We both felt a small crowd (ghosts) form around us.

As I asked her if she would be available later for an interview, I began feeling severe tingling throughout my body (electrified). As we left, I said out loud, "stay here, I know you are with me, I'll be back later."

Chapter 26
UFOs and Abduction Theory

Illustration by Creative Commons

Chapter 26
UFOs and Abduction Theory

PHENOMENA

We live in an age, thanks to television programming and newsprint articles, where people are speaking and feeling safer about discussing their paranormal and perceived UFO craft viewing and/or alien abduction-visitations. Especially now, year 2022, there seems to be a lot of discussion and hype about "what is" or "is not" paranormal.

Although you cannot believe everything you see on television, read in the newspaper, or hear from other sources, there is "some" truth to other's mission in informing the public about the unknown. I for one, am the host-producer of a popular podcast called, Paranormal Encounters Podcast Series. My mission is to educate, entertain, and intrigue. I spend a lot of time interviewing guests while sharing my own personal stories about my perceived paranormal-alien encounters.

Do you believe we alone in this universe? Most would say, "no." However, some, who are skeptical might believe otherwise. Many of us, who are believers, know we are not alone but cannot directly prove it. Why? Because our experiences are often individualized and happen quickly. Not easy to prove in all cases.

Do you believe there are planets out there with habitants just like us? Your answer might be "probably." Habitants? "Yes" ... but just like us, "not necessarily." Some of these inhabitants may be far more or less advanced.

Some people feel they have been visited by aliens in various locations. Some feel they have been abducted. Others, who felt visited, also believed they were downloaded with information from the alien(s). Individuals with contact in any degree would refer to themselves as being a "contactee" or "experiencer".

QUESTIONNAIRE
Written By Kathleen Marden, Director, MUFON
Book Entitled, "Extraterrestrial Contact: What To Do If You've Been ABDUCTED" (2019)

For those of you who believe you may be a "contactee" or "experiencer", take a minute to answer the following questions.

1. Have you observed a UFO craft?
2. Was this UFO craft 500 feet or less away from you?
3. Do you remember seeing NHI (non-human intelligence) entities?
4. Were you alone, or were other people with you? if other people were present, what do they recall?
5. Did you suddenly find yourself in a different location?

6. Have you experienced missing time while you were outside? If so, what do you recall?
7. Was there any evidence such as marks on your body or a problem with your clothing?
8. Have you had recurring dreams about this experience?
9. Have you told anyone about your experience? If so, what was their reaction?
10. If other people ridiculed you after hearing your story, have you spoken with a non-judgmental listener such as a member of a MUFON research team who will not ridicule you?

UFO WATCHING

My husband and I went UFO watching late March 2022 in Sedona, Arizona. Perfect night sky. Clear. Our guide was a well-known contactee' by the name of Michael O'Sedona.

We watched the night sky near the Sedona airport. We used military night vision goggles (best available) for viewing.

We saw many unidentified crafts flying about. Some were satellites, others were military, some may have been extraterrestrial.

Will we ever know the truth behind UFO crafts? At this time, what we saw remains inconclusive.

Chapter 27
4-1-1 Disappearances

Artwork by Kelly Renee Schutz
Illustrative, Location Does Not Infer An Abduction Site

Chapter 27
4-1-1 Disappearances

PHENOMENA

I am fascinated by this topic. You always hear, "don't be the last person wandering in your group as you might suddenly disappear." Creepy. Well, someone is usually the last one in a group (namely, me). How about when you are part of a group and still go missing? And never return. I think this is even more creepy.

In speaking to a few researchers about this topic, some feel the phenomena has an association with something that is "not from our world." According to a description found on the Internet, "missing 411 cases are a colloquial classification that documents missing person cases that fit several criteria." It goes on to infer most disappearances appear to be occurring in a national park, rural area, or large reserve of public land.

It sums up its theory by stating "exceptionally odd circumstances surround the disappearance." If I were to provide two examples for clarity – (1) a person is part of a group wandering on a trail and suddenly, the person who is behind the group in the back disappears; (2) you are walking as part of a group and someone "within" the group next to you suddenly disappears.

In the case of Missing 411, the explanation to these disappearances could be something else. Namely, (1) paranormal, (2) extraterrestrial, (3) cryptid, (4) portal opening, or (5) unusual spot and timing, parallel universe.

According to retired police officer David Paulides, he noticed similarities in unsolved disappearances occurring near National Parks. One common trait is that NONE of the victims left behind a scent trail for search dogs to find.

DISAPPEARANCES

1. The disappearance occurred in a national park, rural area, or large reserve of public land.
2. Exceptionally odd circumstances surround the disappearance.
3. Mental illness or voluntary disappearance does not appear to be the cause.

TRUE INCIDENTS

Although there are several incidents, here are two that made me sick to my stomach.

INCIDENTS #1 and #2 – (1) Young boy missing from his family (split second). Seen in distance on the shoulders of a sasquatch being carried off going towards forest but disappears into mid-air. No one knows how boy was abducted. Boy never seen again. (2) Young boy goes missing. Discovered on a flat rock in swamp. Clothes removed. Clothes folded sitting next to him. Boy is dead.

Guest Interviews and Features
Paranormal-Extraterrestrial Experiencer

AMAZON (11 BOOKS) – MOST POPULAR and KINDLE
Haunted Life: Unable to Hide = just launched Amazon
Message Received = www.amazon.com/dp/B091WGH7HX (Both)
Manifestations = www.amazon.com/dp/179413414X (no Kindle)

FEATURED WORKSHOP SPEAKER, PRESENTER, and BOOTH
4th UFO Mega Conference, pending new date/location   **2023**
Speaker: "Haunted Life: Stalked by Unexplained Paranormal-
Extraterrestrial Pests" (2½ hours); meet-greet; ticket purchase

2nd MN ParaUnity Conv, Mystic Lake Casino   **Sept 29-Oct 1, 2022**
Vendor Booth and Presenter (1 hour), title is pending

Metaphysical & Paranormal Expo, Janesville, WI   **Apr 8-10, 2022**
Vendor Booth

HOST-PRODUCER: PODCAST, RADIO AFFLILIATIONS
Paranormal Encounters Podcast Series [Podomatic]	**began 2016**
Para-X Radio Network [paraxradionetwork.com]	**began 2017**
KPNL Radio, Ohio [kpnl-db.com]	**pending**

RADIO INTERVIEWS - Hosted By
Yaya Diamond Dream Chasers Radio™, Florida	**01-23-2022**
The Zach Feldman Show (ZRadioLive), New York	**01-19-2022**
Para-X Radio Network w/Erick Bee, Pennsylvania	**02-27-2017**
Darkness Radio w/Dave Schrader & Tim Dennis, MN	**08-10-2016**

PODCAST INTERVIEWS-VIDEO APPEARANCES – Hosted By
Ghostly Talk Radio w/Scott L. & Amber, Michigan	**03-19-2022**
Pursuit of the Paranormal w/Ash and Greg, England	**02-21-2022**
P.E.E.P. w/Niki Morock, North Carolina	**02-16-2022**
Guy Who Knows A Guy w/Michael Whitehouse, CT	**02-05-2022**
Paranormal Connection w/Joe Foster, Arkansas	**02-03-2022**
Paranormal Portal w/Brent Thomas, Idaho	**01-30-2022**
Paranormal Heart w/Kat Ward, Canada	**01-30-2022**
Influence Spotlight w/Chris Templeton, Los Angeles	**01-06-2022**
Panel: Power Lunch Live w/Michael Whitehouse, CT	**01-28-2022**
Behind the Pen w/Karina Kantas, Greece	**01-12-2022**
B-52 Burgers and Brew Restaurant, Minnesota	**03-15-2020**

AUTHOR FEATURES: MAGAZINE, ARTICLES, BOOK BLOGS

Writer's Life Magazine, 2-Page, by LaDonna Smith   03-01-2022

Author and Blog Features (lengthy), by Abantika Bose   01-23-2022

Author Feature (Spot) written by Carla Dempsey   01-15-2022

Dr. Mel's Message, Book Blog, by Dr. Melissa Caudle   01-13-2022

BOOK 1. 235 Pages. **Topics** = Death, Superstitions, Ghost Attractions, Hauntings. **Personal Stories** = 12 Illustrated Real-Life Stories. **Bonus** = Investigator Theoretical Tool Kit, Equipment, and Debunking Paranormal Experiences.

BOOK 2. 254 Pages. **Topics** = Angels, Demons, Ghost Animals, Portals. **Personal Stories** = 12 Illustrated Real-Life Stories. **Bonus** = Investigator Theoretical Tool Kit, Equipment, and Debunking Paranormal Experiences.

BOOK 3. 306 Pages. There are NO topics in this book. This book combines 24 stories from Book 1 and Book 2. **Bonus** = Investigator Theoretical Tool Kit, Equipment, and Debunking Paranormal Experiences.

331

BOOK 4. 202 Pages. **Topics** = Dreams, Near Death, Death, Superstitions, Angels, Demons, Ghost Animals, Psychics, Ghost Attractions, Hauntings, Moon Phases and Energy Fields, Orbs and Vortexes, Portals, Spectral Sites. **Bonus** = Investigator Theoretical Tool Kit, Equipment, and Debunking Paranormal Experiences.

PARANORMAL
ENCOUNTERS
HANGING AROUND

KELLY RENEE SCHUTZ
Illustrated Paranormal Stories

BOOK 5. 318 Pages. This book contains 5 fiction (not real) and 20 non-fiction (real) paranormal stories. **Bonus** = Debunking Paranormal Experiences.

333

BOOK 6. 160 Pages. This book contains fiction, non-fiction, and children's interpretations (short) on their ghost experiences. **Bonus** = Adult Stories and Debunking Paranormal Experiences.

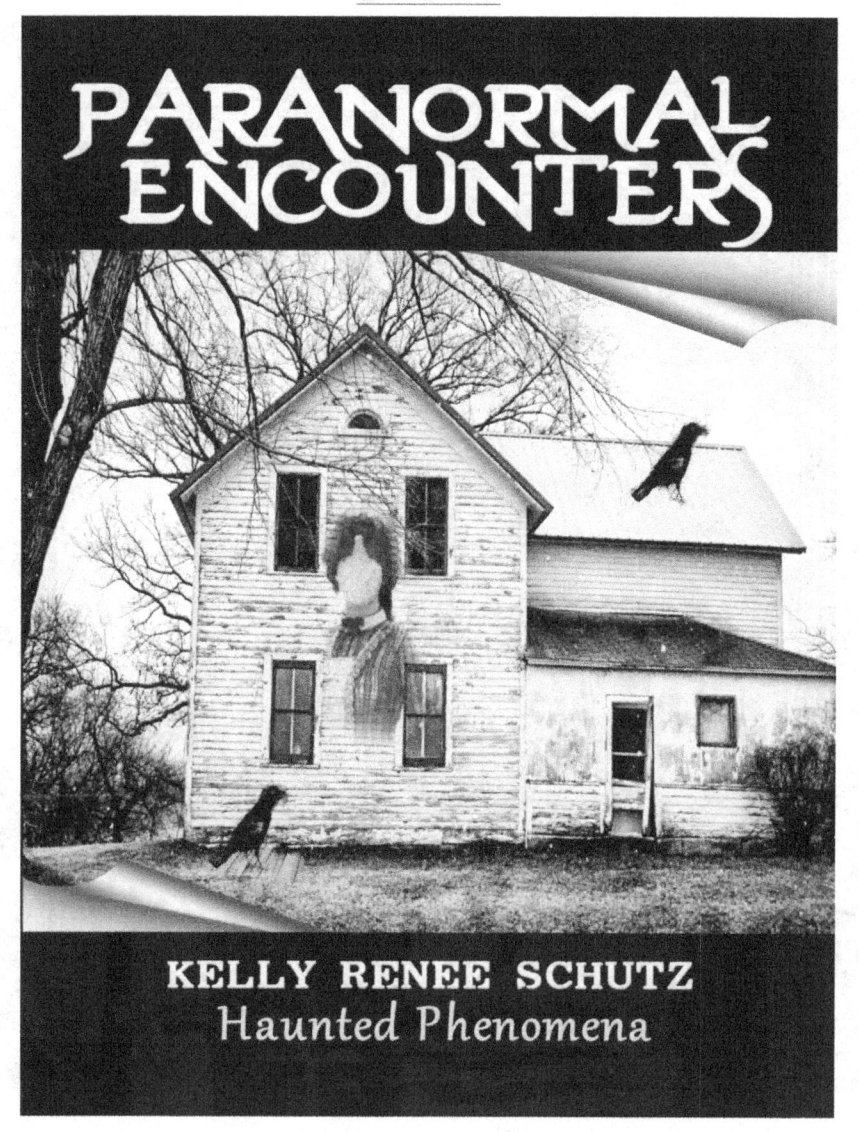

PARANORMAL ENCOUNTERS

KELLY RENEE SCHUTZ
Haunted Phenomena

BOOK 7. 200 Pages. This book compiles all stories from Books 1-6 (short versions). 70+ non-fiction paranormal experiences. **Bonus** = Debunking Paranormal Experience.
335

INVESTIGATIVE JOURNAL

PARANORMAL ACTIVITY

KELLY SCHUTZ

BOOK 8. 80 Pages. This journal is designed as a notebook to collect experiences. Toward the end, it contains the Investigator Theoretical Tool Kit, Checklist for Conditions, and Debunking Paranormal Experiences.

BOOK 9. 381 Pages. This book compiles 31 stories from Books 1-3 and 5 (popular). Illustrated.

BOOK 10. 363 Pages. This book contains 20 stories from the author's first-hand accounts with paranormal-supernatural activity including a few stories from contributors. Illustrated.

338

BOOK 11. 383 Pages. This book contains 18 non-fiction (author experiences), 5 fiction, and 4 topics of interest. Recommended Combo Purchases: Book 9 and 11 (3 repetitive chapters) **or** Book 10 and 11 (5 repetitive).

Paranormal Encounters
Podcast Series

Podcasts and Worldwide Interviews

> ## PODCASTS HEARD WORLDWIDE

SUBSCRIBE FOR FREE

http://krschutz1paranormalencounters.podomatic.com

OR www.paranormaluniveralpress.com

Also find me at:

www.podomatic.com/podcasts/krschutz1paranormalencounters.

The Paranormal Encounters Podcast Series gives credit to my guests, artists, and music composers. Maynard and Mildred add a special contribution. Special credit given to Elliot Shulman, New Jersey, my pre-show announcer. On my webpage – go to upper right, click on Podomatic tab.

Paranormal Phenomena Snips
Books 1-9

Defying Naturalism

Through A Childs Eyes

Hanging Around

Beyond the Grave

Defying Naturalism

343

Beyond the Grave

Through a Child's Eyes

Through a Child's Eyes

Through a Child's Eyes

Music Composer
Vitaliy Hava, Burshtyn City, Ukraine

Vitaliy Hava resides in Burshtyn City, Ukraine. He has more than 10 years of experience in audio production as a freelancer and has worked with clients all over the globe on original soundtracks for computer games, cartoons, music for television, podcasts, music albums, and radio commercials. He had worked for Garbuz Studio, where he had a chance to master his skills on audio production while delivering high quality projects under strict deadlines. He currently owns his own studio. Contact him thru **upwork.com or vitaliy.hava@gmail.com.**

Music Composer
Evgeny Ryabovol, Kherson, Ukraine

Evgeny Ryabovol resides in Kherson, Ukraine. He studied hydrotechnology at Kherson Agricultural University and earned a diploma as an expert engineer. He became interested in music around the age of 15, initially as a hobby. In 2005, he had a metal-band in which he was the lead singer and guitarist. After five years, the band broke up and Evgeny went on to write and compose music where he has worked to master the principles of sound recording, mixing, mastering and sound design. Contact him thru **upwork.com**.   347

Music Composer

Jonatan Alberto Arriaga Zaragoza
Mexico City, Mexico

Jonatan Alberto Arriaga Zaragoza resides just outside of Mexico City, Mexico. He has more than five years of experience with sound design and music composition, particularly for the media and songwriting. He loves to score cinematic cues and has experience working with sampled instruments through Native Instruments´ Kontakt. He enjoys creating sounds and music for video games. Currently, he is taking a certification course for WWise middleware. He may be contacted **thru upwork.com.**

Music Composer
Elliott McLaughlin, London, England

Elliott McLaughlin resides in London, England. He is a UK based composer, producer, and songwriter for CLIMBR, featuring contemporary, memorable, and exquisitely polished compositions. He has explored music since an early age. Studied at the Leeds College of Music. From live band multi-instrumentalist, to composer, producer, and DJ, CLIMBR is on a journey to triumph every challenge that music has to offer. A prestigious degree in music production along with years of professional experience, CLIMBR is versatile, dynamic and forward-thinking producer with an expert standard of composition and engineering. Contact him thru **upwork.com**.

Music Composer
Franco Luciano Donatti
Buenos Aires, Argentina

Franco Luciano Donatti resides in Buenos Aires, Argentina. He started to play the piano at the age of 15 years old. Around 2012, he has studied the mastery of arts, a degree in piano at the Buenos Aires National Conservatory. From 2015, he has been studying musical composition at the University of Arts in Buenos Aires. He has composed several music compositions for audiovisuals and video games as well as recorded piano music as a sideman musician. He is currently creating his studio called "Techno Classics1", which aims to create audio production for film scores, video games music, and audio recordings. Contact him thru **upwork.com**.

Music Composer
Phil Michalski, Manchester, United Kingdom

Phil Michalski was born in Warsaw, Poland. He currently resides in Manchester, United Kingdom. In 2007, he graduated from the Academy of Film and TV with a major in sound engineering. Since then, he had worked for the biggest radio station in Poland, "Poland National Radio," as a producer, sound engineer, and composer. In 2013, he moved to the United Kingdom and established a small post-production business called AudioPhil, where he currently works as a senior producer for a multiple parsec award-winning podcast, the *NoSleep* podcast. Phil's passion is sound design. He loves to record everything that makes a sound and processes his recording into new sounds. Contact him thru **http://philmichalski.com.**

Be Careful What You Wish For

Made in the USA
Monee, IL
10 February 2025

11825053R00213